FOREWORD

"The American Way of Life" . . . how often do we hear these words? How often do we read them?

What is the American Way of Life, and what does it mean to those of us fortunate enough to have the opportunity of living it?

Heritage Publishers, Inc., believe that it is embodied in the principles of liberty and justice, and in the sacrifices, the hardships, the "blood, sweat, and tears" of those Americans, both the famous and the unknown, who have worked and fought to make these principles a reality. Our forefathers founded this country because of their burning desire to achieve liberty and freedom, and they fought their mother country in order to secure them and make them endure. How they accomplished these purposes in vividly illustrated in the documents reproduced in this book.

It is the opinion of the editors that the reading and rereading of the Documents of Our Heritage will give everyone, student and non-student alike, an insight into the making of our history and an enhanced appreciation of the remarkable achievements of those who have helped make our history. These documents are not mere historic curios: they represent the heritage of all Americans and demonstrate the spirit of free men everywhere.

HERITAGE PUBLISHERS, INC.
Memphis, Tennessee.

The Historic Documents contained herein are reproduced by special arrangement with the American Heritage Foundation, sponsor of the Freedom Train (1947 - 1948)

Epistola Christofori Colom: cui etas nostra multũ debet: de Insulis Indie supra Gangem nuper inuẽtis·Ad quas pergren/ das octauo antea mense auspiciis τ ere inuictissimoꝗ Fernãdi τ Helisabet Hispaniaꝗ Regũ missus fuerat: ad magnificum dñm Gabrielem Sanchis eorundẽ serenissimoꝗ Regum Tesaurariũ missa:quã nobilis ac litteratus vir Leander de Cosco ab Hispa no idiomate in latinum conuertit tertio kal's Maii·M·cccc·xciii Pontificatus Alexandri Sexti Anno primo·

Quoniam suscepte prouintie rem perfectam me prosecutum fuisse gratum tibi fore scio:has constitui exarare: que te vniuscuiusꝗ rei in hoc nostro itinere geste inuenteꝗ ad moneant:Tricesimotertio die postꝗ Gadibus discessi in mare Indicũ perueni:vbi plurimas insulas innumeris habitatas ho minibus repperi:quarum omnium pro felicissimo Rege nostro preconio celebrato τ vexillis extensis contradicente nemine pos sessionem accepi:primeꝗ earum diui Saluatoris nomen impo/ sui:cuius fretus auxilio tam ad hanc:ꝗ ad ceteras alias perue/ nimus·Eam ꝟo Indi Guanahanin vocant·Aliarũ etiam vnam quanꝗ nouo nomine nuncupaui: quippe aliã insulam Sancte Marie Conceptionis·aliam Fernandinam·aliam Hysabellam· aliam Joanam·τ sic de reliquis appellari iussi·Cum primum in eam insulam quam dudum Joanam vocari dixi appulimus: iu xta eius littus occidentem versus aliquantulum processi: tamꝗ eam magnam nullo reperto fine inueni:vt non insulã: sed conti nentem Chatai prouinciam esse crediderim: nulla tñ videns op pida municipiaue in maritimis sita confinib? preter aliquos vi cos τ predia rustica:cum quoꝗ incolis loqui nequibam·quare si mul ac nos videbant surripiebant fugam·progrediebar vltra: existimans aliquã me vrbem villasue inuenturũ·Deniꝗ videns ꝗ longe admodum progressis nihil noui emergebat:τ bmõi via nos ad Septentrionem deferebat:ꝗ ipse fugere exoptabã:terris etenim regnabat bruma:ad Austrumꝗ erat in voto cõtendere·

rit opus·tñ vero aromatum·bombicis·masticis:ꝗ apud Chium duntaxat innenitur·tantũꝗ ligni aloes·tantum seruoꝗ bydo/ latrarum:quantum eorum maiestas voluerit exigere·it.m reus barbarum τ alia aromatum genera que ii quos in dicta arce reli qui iam inuenisse atꝗ inuenturos existimo·ꝗñquidem ego nul libi magis sum moratus nisi quantum me coegerunt venti:pre teriꝗ in villa Natiuitatis:dum arcez condere τ tuta oĩa esse pro uidi·Que τ si maxima τ inaudita sunt:multo tñ maiora forent si naues mihi vt ratio exigit subuenissent·Veꝗ multum ac mira bile hoc:nec nostris meritis correspondens:sed sancte Christia/ ne fidei:nostrorumꝗ Regum pietati ac religioni:quia quod hu manus consequi nõ poterat intellectus:id humanis cõcessit di uinus·Solet enim deus seruus suos:quiꝗ sua precepta diligũt τ in impossibilibus exaudire:vt nobis in presentia contigit:qui ea consecuti sumus que hactenus mortalium vires minime atti gerant:nam si harũ insulaꝗ quipiam aliquid scripserunt aut lo cuti sunt:omnes per ambages τ coiecturas·nemo se eas vidisse asserit vnde prope videbatur fabula·Igitur Rex τ Regina prin cepsꝗ ac eoꝗ regna felicissima cuncteꝗ alie Christianoꝗ prouin cie Saluatori dño nostro Jesu Christo agamꝰ gratias: qui tan ta nos victoria munereꝗ donauit:celebrentur processiones·per agantur solennia sacra:festaꝗ fronde velentur delubra·exultet Christus in terris quemadmodum in celis exultat:quom tot po pulorum perditas ante hac animas saluatum iri preuidet·Lete mur τ nos:cum propter exaltationem nostre fidei·tum propter rerum temporalium incrementa:quoꝗ non solum Hispania sed vniuersa Christianitas est futura particeps·Hec vt gesta sunt sic breuiter enarrata·Vale·Vlisbone pridie Idus Martii·

Christoforus Colom Oceane classis Prefectus·

Letter by Christopher Columbus on the Discovery of America (1493)

On returning from his first voyage, Columbus wrote an official letter to Gabriel Sanchez, crown treasurer of the King and Queen of Spain, Ferdinand and Isabella, announcing his discovery. This tremendous news was immediately put into print and swept through Europe. Editions appeared in Latin, Italian and German. This is a copy of the second Latin edition, printed in Rome in 1493. A partial translation follows: "Thirty-three days after my departure from Cadiz, I reached the Indian sea, where I discovered many islands, thickly peopled, of which I took possession without resistance in the name of our most illustrious Monarch, by public procla- mation and with unfurled banners. To the first of these islands, which is called by the Indians Guanahani, I gave the name of the blessed Saviour (San Salvador), relying upon whose protection I had reached this as well as the other islands; to each of these I also gave a name, ordering that one should be called Santa Maria de la Concepción, another Fernandina, the third Isabella, the fourth Juana (Cuba)."

" - - - and found it to be so large and apparently without termination, that I cannot suppose it to be an island but the continental province of Cathay. Seeing however no towns or populous places on the seacoast but only a few detached houses and cottages with whose inhabitants I was unable to communicate, because they fled as soon as they saw us - - - ."

Lent to The Freedom Train by Mrs. Marshall Ludington Brown and the Princeton University Library

the South of the Cape, but at night the winde being con-
trary, we put round againe for the Bay of *Cape Cod* : and
vpon the 11. of *Nouember*, we came to an anchor in the
Bay, which is a good harbour and pleasant Bay, circled
round, except in the entrance, which is about foure miles
ouer from land to land, compassed about to the very Sea
with Okes, Pines, Iuniper, Sassafras, and other sweet wood;
it is a harbour wherein 1000. saile of Ships may safely ride,
there we relieued our selues with wood and water, and re-
freshed our people, while our shallop was fitted to coast the
Bay, to search for an habitation: there was the greatest store
of fowle that euer we saw.

And euery day we saw Whales playing hard by vs, of
which in that place, if we had instruments & meanes to take
them, we might haue made a very rich returne, which to
our great griefe we wanted. Our master and his mate, and
others experienced in fishing, professed, we might haue
made three or foure thousand pounds worth of Oyle; they
preferred it before Greenland Whale-fishing, & purpose the
next winter to fish for Whale here ; for Cod we assayed, but
found none, there is good store no doubt in their season.
Neither got we any fish all the time we lay there, but some
few little ones on the shore. We found great Mussles, and
very fat and full of Sea pearle, but we could not eat them,
for they made vs all sicke that did eat, as well saylers as pas-
sengers ; they caused to cast and secure, but they were soone
well againe. The bay is so round & circling, that before we
could come to anchor, we went round all the points of the
Compasse. We could not come neere the shore by three
quarters of an English mile, because of shallow water,
which was a great preiudice to vs, for our people going on
shore were forced to wade a bow shoot or two in going a-
land, which caused many to get colds and coughs, for it was
many times freezing cold weather.

This day before we came to harbour, obseruing some not
well affected to vnitie and concord, but gaue some appea-
rance of faction, it was thought good there should be an association and agreement, that we should combine together
in

in one body, and to submit to such government and gover-
nours, as we should by common consent agree to make and
chose, and set our hands to this that followes word for
word.

IN the name of God, Amen. We whose names are vnder-
written, the loyall Subiects of our dread soueraigne Lord
King IAMES, by the grace of God of Great *Britaine, France,*
and *Ireland* King, Defender of the Faith, &c.

Hauing vnder-taken for the glory of God, and advance-
ment of the Christian Faith, and honour of our King and
Countrey, a Voyage to plant the first Colony in the Nor-
therne parts of VIRGINIA, doe by these presents solemnly
& mutually in the presence of *God* and one of another, coue-
nant, and combine our selues together into a civill body po-
litike, for our better ordering and preseruation, and furthe-
rance of the ends aforesaid ; and by vertue hereof to enact, constitute, and frame such iust and equall Lawes, Ordinances, acts, constitutions, offices from time to time, as shall
be thought most meet and convenient for the generall good
of the Colony: vnto which we promise all due submission
and obedience. In witnesse whereof we haue here vnder
subscribed our names *Cape Cod* 11. of *Nouember*, in the yeare
of the raigne of our soueraigne Lord King IAMES, of *England, France,* and *Ireland* 18. and of *Scotland* 54. *Anno Do-
mino* 1620.

The same day so soone as we could we set a-shore 15. or
16. men, well armed, with some to fetch wood, for we had
none left ; as also to see what the Land was, and what Inhabitants they could meet with, they found it to be a small neck
of Land ; on this side where we lay is the *Bay,* and the further
side the Sea ; the ground or earth, sand hils, much like the
Downes in *Holland,* but much better ; the crust of the earth a
Spits depth, excellent blacke earth ; all wooded with Okes,
Pines, Sassafras, Iuniper, Birch, Holly, Vines, some Ash, Wal-
nut ; the wood for the most part open and without vnder-
wood, fit either to goe or ride in : at night our people returned,

C 2

The Mayflower Compact (1620)

Before landing from the "Mayflower" the Pilgrims drew up a compact which provided for their government during the first years of the Plymouth Colony. This copy is the text as published in John Mourt's **Relation** of 1622, the first account printed in England of the voyage of the Pilgrims.

Lent to The Freedom Train by the Library of Congress

Congress OF THE United States,

begun and held at the City of New York, on

Wednesday, the fourth of March, one thousand seven hundred and eighty nine.

THE Conventions of a number of the States having, at the time of their adopting the Constitution, expressed a desire, in order to prevent misconstruction or abuse of its powers, that further declaratory and restrictive clauses should be added: And as extending the ground of public confidence in the Government, will best ensure the beneficent ends of its institution.

RESOLVED, by the Senate and House of Representatives of the United States of America in Congress assembled, two thirds of both Houses concurring, that the following Articles be proposed to the Legislatures of the several States, as Amendments to the Constitution of the United States, all or any of which Articles, when ratified by three fourths of the said Legislatures, to be valid to all intents and purposes, as part of the said Constitution; viz.

ARTICLES in addition to, and amendment of the Constitution of the United States of America, proposed by Congress, and ratified by the Legislatures of the several States, pursuant to the fifth Article of the original Constitution.

Article the first. After the first enumeration required by the first Article of the Constitution, there shall be one Representative for every thirty thousand, until the number shall amount to one hundred, after which the proportion shall be so regulated by Congress, that there shall be not less than one hundred Representatives, nor less than one Representative for every forty thousand persons, until the number of Representatives shall amount to two hundred, after which the proportion shall be so regulated by Congress, that there shall not be less than two hundred Representatives, nor more than one Representative for every fifty thousand persons.

Article the second. No law, varying the compensation for the services of the Senators and Representatives, shall take effect, until an election of Representatives shall have intervened.

Article the third. Congress shall make no law respecting an establishment of religion, or prohibiting the free exercise thereof; or abridging the freedom of speech, or of the press; or the right of the people peaceably to assemble, and to petition the Government for a redress of grievances.

Article the fourth. A well regulated Militia, being necessary to the security of a free State, the right of the people to keep and bear Arms, shall not be infringed.

Article the fifth. No soldier shall, in time of peace be quartered in any house, without the consent of the owner, nor in time of war, but in a manner to be prescribed by law.

Article the sixth. The right of the people to be secure in their persons, houses, papers, and effects, against unreasonable searches and seizures, shall not be violated, and no warrants shall issue, but upon probable cause, supported by oath or affirmation, and particularly describing the place to be searched, and the persons or things to be seized.

Article the seventh. No person shall be held to answer for a capital, or otherwise infamous crime, unless on a presentment or indictment of a grand jury, except in cases arising in the land or naval forces, or in the Militia, when in actual service in time of War or public danger; nor shall any person be subject for the same offence to be twice put in jeopardy of life or limb; nor shall be compelled in any criminal case, to be a witness against himself, nor be deprived of life, liberty, or property, without due process of law; nor shall private property be taken for public use, without just compensation.

Article the eighth. In all criminal prosecutions, the accused shall enjoy the right to a speedy and public trial, by an impartial jury of the State and district wherein the crime shall have been committed, which district shall have been previously ascertained by law, and to be informed of the nature and cause of the accusation; to be confronted with the witnesses against him; to have compulsory process for obtaining witnesses in his favor, and to have the assistance of counsel for his defence.

Article the ninth. In suits at common law, where the value in controversy shall exceed twenty dollars, the right of trial by jury shall be preserved, and no fact tried by a jury, shall be otherwise re-examined in any Court of the United States, than according to the rules of the common law.

Article the tenth. Excessive bail shall not be required, nor excessive fines imposed, nor cruel and unusual punishments inflicted.

Article the eleventh. The enumeration in the Constitution, of certain rights, shall not be construed to deny or disparage others retained by the people.

Article the twelfth. The powers not delegated to the United States by the Constitution, nor prohibited by it to the States, are reserved to the States respectively, or to the people.

Frederick Augustus Muhlenberg, *Speaker of the House of Representatives.*

John Adams, *Vice President of the United States, and President of the Senate.*

ATTEST,

John Beckley, *Clerk of the House of Representatives.*

Sam. A. Otis *Secretary of the Senate.*

The Bill of Rights (1789)

In the Bill of Rights, the first ten amendments to the Constitution, protection of those "unalienable rights" asserted so eloquently in the Declaration of Independence, was written into the fundamental law of the land. The document known as the Bill of Rights, guaranteeing such precious liberties as freedom of speech, freedom of religion, and freedom of the press, is the joint resolution of Congress of September 25, 1789, proposing 12 amendments, only 10 of which were ratified and in 1791 became a part of the Constitution. It is inscribed on parchment and is signed by Frederick Augustus Muhlenberg, Speaker of the House of Representatives, and John Adams, Vice President of the United States and President of the Senate. Faded though the writing be and yellow the parchment, this original document symbolizes the extraordinary personal and civil liberties that are a cherished part of our American heritage.

Lent to The Freedom Train by the National Archives

presentatives, shall have authority to make laws in all cases for the good government of the district, not repugnant to the principles and articles in this ordinance established and declared. And all bills having passed by a majority in the house, and by a majority in the council, shall be referred to the governor for his assent; but no bill or legislative act whatever, shall be of any force without his assent. The governor shall have power to convene, prorogue and dissolve the general assembly, when in his opinion it shall be expedient.

The governor, judges, legislative council, secretary, and such other officers as Congress shall appoint in the district, shall take an oath or affirmation of fidelity, and of office, the governor before the president of Congress, and all other officers before the governor. As soon as a legislature shall be formed in the district, the council and house, assembled in one room, shall have authority by joint ballot to elect a delegate to Congress, who shall have a seat in Congress, with a right of debating, but not of voting, during this temporary government.

And for extending the fundamental principles of civil and religious liberty, which form the basis whereon these republics, their laws and constitutions are erected; to fix and establish those principles as the basis of all laws, constitutions and governments, which forever hereafter shall be formed in the said territory;—to provide also for the establishment of states, and permanent government therein, and for their admission to a share in the federal councils on an equal footing with the original states, at as early periods as may be consistent with the general interest:

It is hereby ordained and declared by the authority aforesaid, That the following articles shall be considered as articles of compact between the original states and the people and states in the said territory, and forever remain unalterable, unless by common consent, to wit:

Article the First. No person, demeaning himself in a peaceable and orderly manner, shall ever be molested on account of his mode of worship or religious sentiments in the said territory.

Article the Second. The inhabitants of the said territory shall always be entitled to the benefits of the writ of habeas corpus, and of the trial by jury; of a proportionate representation of the people in the legislature, and of judicial proceedings according to the course of the common law; all persons shall be bailable unless for capital offences, where the proof shall be evident, or the presumption great; all fines shall be moderate, and no cruel or unusual punishments shall be inflicted; no man shall be deprived of his liberty or property but by the judgment of his peers, or the law of the land; and should the public exigencies make it necessary for the common preservation to take any person's property, or to demand his particular services, full compensation shall be made for the same; — and in the just preservation of rights and property it is understood and declared, that no law ought ever to be made, or have force in the said territory, that shall in any manner whatever interfere with, or affect private contracts or engagements, bona fide and without fraud previously formed.

Article the Third. Religion, morality and knowledge, being necessary to good government and the happiness of mankind, schools and the means of education shall forever be encouraged. The utmost good faith shall always be observed towards the Indians; their lands and property shall never be taken from them without their consent; and in their property, rights and liberty, they never shall be invaded or disturbed, unless in just and lawful wars authorised by Congress; but laws founded in justice and humanity shall from time to time be made, for preventing wrongs being done to them, and for preserving peace and friendship with them.

Article the Fourth. The said territory, and the states which may be formed therein, shall forever remain a part of this confederacy of the United States of America, subject to the articles of confederation, and to such alterations therein as shall be constitutionally made; and to all the acts and ordinances of the United states in Congress assembled, conformable thereto. The inhabitants and settlers in the said territory, shall be subject to pay a part of the federal debts contracted or to be contracted, and a proportional part of the expences of government, to be apportioned on them by Congress, according to the same common rule and measure by which apportionments thereof shall be made on the other states; and the taxes for paying their proportion, shall be laid and levied by the authority and direction of the legislatures of the district or districts or new states, as in the original states, within the time agreed upon by the United States in Congress assembled. The legislatures of those districts, or new states, shall never interfere with the primary disposal of the soil by the United States in Congress assembled, nor with any regulations Congress may find necessary for securing the title in such soil to the bona fide purchasers. No tax shall be imposed on lands the property of the United States; and in no case shall non-resident proprietors be taxed higher than residents. The navigable waters leading into the Mississippi and St. Lawrence, and the carrying places between the same shall be common highways, and forever free, as well to the inhabitants of the said territory, as to the citizens of the United States, and those of any other states that may be admitted into the confederacy, without any tax, impost or duty therefor.

Article the Fifth. There shall be formed in the said territory, not less than three nor more than five states; and the boundaries of the states, as soon as Virginia shall alter her act of cession and consent to the same, shall become fixed and established as follows: The western state in the said territory, shall be bounded by the Mississippi, the Ohio and Wabash rivers; a direct line drawn from the Wabash and Post Vincent's due north to the territorial line between the United States and Canada, and by the said territorial line to the lake of the Woods and Mississippi. The middle state shall be bounded by the said direct line, the Wabash from Post Vincent's to the Ohio; by the Ohio, by a direct line drawn due north from the mouth of the Great Miami to the said territorial line, and by the said territorial line. The eastern state shall be bounded by the last mentioned direct line, the Ohio, Pennsylvania, and the said territorial line; Provided however, and it is further understood and declared, that the boundaries of these three states, shall be subject so far to be altered, that if Congress shall hereafter find it expedient, they shall have authority to form one or two states in that part of the said territory which lies north of an east and west line drawn through the southerly bend or extreme of lake Michigan: and whenever any of the said states shall have sixty thousand free inhabitants therein, such state shall be admitted by its delegates into the Congress of the United states, on an equal footing with the original states in all respects whatever; and shall be at liberty to form a permanent constitution and state government: Provided the constitution and government so to be formed, shall be republican, and in conformity to the principles contained in these articles; and so far as it can be consistent with the general interest of the confederacy, such admission shall be allowed at an earlier period, and when there may be a less number of free inhabitants in the state than sixty thousand.

Article the Sixth. There shall be neither slavery nor involuntary servitude in the said territory, otherwise than in punishment of crimes whereof the party shall have been duly convicted: Provided always, that any person escaping into the same, from whom labor or service is lawfully claimed in any one of the original states, such fugitive may be lawfully reclaimed and conveyed to the person claiming his or her labor or service as aforesaid.

Be it ordained by the authority aforesaid, That the resolutions of the 23d of April, 1784, relative to the subject of this ordinance, be, and the same are hereby repealed and declared null and void.

DONE by the UNITED STATES in CONGRESS assembled, the 13th day of July, in the year of our Lord 1787, and of their sovereignty and independence the 12th.

Cha Thomson secy

The Northwest Ordinance (1787)

The printed text of the Ordinance, signed by Charles Thomson, Secretary of the Congress, is from records of the Northwest Territory. The Northwest Ordinance is also a landmark in the progress of education in the United States. "Religion, morality, and knowledge being necessary to good government and the happiness of mankind, schools and the means of education shall forever be encouraged," it states. The States formed, in whole or part, from the Northwest Territory are: Ohio (1803), Indiana (1816), Illinois (1818), Michigan (1837), and Wisconsin (1848).

THE
VVHOLE
BOOKE OF PSALMES
Faithfully
TRANSLATED *into* ENGLISH
Metre.

Whereunto is prefixed a difcourfe declaring not only the lawfullnes, but alfo
the neceffity of the heavenly Ordinance
of finging Scripture Pfalmes in
the Churches of
God.

Coll. III.
*Let the word of God dwell plenteoufly in
you, in all wifdome, teaching and exhort-
ing one another in Pfalmes, Himnes, and
fpirituall Songs, finging to the Lord with
grace in your hearts.*

Iames v.
*If any be afflicted, let him pray, and if
any be merry let him fing pfalmes.*

Imprinted
1640

First Book Printed in America

Printed by Stephen Daye in 1640 and popularly known as The Bay Psalm Book, it is one of the few surviving copies of the first book printed in the North American Colonies.

Lent to The Freedom Train by Dr. A. S. W. Rosenbach

THE
New-York Weekly JOURNAL

Containing the freſheſt Advices, Foreign, and Domeſtick.

MUNDAY November 25th, 1734.

To all my Subſcribers and Benefactors who take my weekly Journall.

Gentlemen, Ladies and Others;

AS you laſt week were Diſ-appointed of my Journall, I think it Incumbent up-on me, to publiſh my Apoligy which is this. On the Lords Day, the Seventeenth of this Inſtant, I was Arreſted, taken and Impriſoned in the common Gôal of this Citty, by Virtue of a Warrant from the *Governour*, and the Hono-rable *Franciſs Harriſon, Eſq*; and others in Councill of which (God willing) yo'l have a Coppy, whereupon I was put under ſuch Reſtraint that I had not the Liberty of Pen, Ink, or Paper, or to ſee, or ſpeak with People, till upon my Complaint to the Honôurable the Chief Juſtice, at my appearing before him upon my *Habias Corpus* on the *Wedneſday* following. Who diſ-countenanced that Proceeding, and therefore I have had ſince that Time, the Liberty of Speaking through the Hole of the Door, to my Wife and Servants by which I doubt not yo'l think me ſufficiently Excuſed for not ſending my laſt weeks *Journall*, and I hope for the future by the Liberty of Speaking to my Servants thro' the Hole of the Door of the Priſon, to entertain you with my weekly *Journal* as formerly. *And am your obliged Humble Servant,* J. Peter Zenger.

Mr. *Zenger*;

AS the Liberty of the Preſs is juſtly eſteemed and univerſally acknowled-ged by Engliſhmen, to be the grand Paladium of all their Liberties, which Liberty of the Preſs, I have rejoyced to ſee well defended in Sundry of your Papers, and particularly by your No. 2. 3. 10. 11. 15. 16. 17. 18. 24. & 54. and by an annonimous Authors Obſervations on the chief Juſtices Charge of *January* laſt ; now, for as much as it may not only be of preſent Uſe, but of future Advantage, that ſuch Matters of Fact, that con-cern the Liberty of the Preſs, may be faithfully recorded and tranſmitted to Poſterity, therefore I have ſent you a Detail of ſuch particulars that con-cern the Liberty of the Preſs within this Colony, and becauſe I would not have you or my ſelf charged with the Publication of a Libel, I ſhall confine my ſelf to a plain Narration of Facts without any comments.

On Tueſday the 15th of Octo. 1734. *The ſupream Court of* New-York, be-gan, when the Honourable James De Lancey, Eſq; *Cheif Juſtie charged the Grand Jury. The Conclusion of which Charge was as follows.*

Gentlemen, I ſhall conclude with reading a Paragraph or two out of the ſame Book, † concerning Libels; they are arrived to that height, that they

ca

THE
Pennfylvania *GAZETTE*.

Containing the frefheft Advices Foreign and Domeftick.

From November 10. to November 17, 1737.

To the AUTHOR of the Pennsylvania
GAZETTE.

SIR,

FREEDOM OF SPEECH is a *principal Pillar* in a free Government: when this Support is taken away, the Conftitution is diffolved, and Tyranny is erected on its ruins. Republicks and limited Monarchies derive their ftrength and vigour from a *Popular Examination* into the Actions of the Magiftrates. This Privilege in all Ages has been and always will be abufed. The beft of Princes could not efcape the cenfure and envy of the times they lived in. But the evil is not fo great as it may appear at firft Sight. A Magiftrate, who fincerely aims at the *Good* of the fociety, will always have the inclinations of a great majority on his fide; and impartial Pofterity will not fail to render him Juftice.

These abuses of the Freedom of Speech are the excrefcencies of Liberty. They ought to be fuppreffed; but to whom dare we commit the care of doing it? An evil Magiftrate, entrufted with a Power to *punifh Words*, is armed with a Weapon the moft *deftructive and terrible*. Under pretence of pruning off the exuberant branches, he frequently deftroys the Tree.

It is certain, that he, who robs another of his moral reputation, more richly merits a Gibbet, than if he had plundered him of his purfe on the high-way. *Auguftus Cæfar* under the fpecious pretext of preferving the characters of the *Romans* from defamation, introduced the Law, whereby *Libelling* was involved in the penalties of *Treason* againft the State. This eftablifhed his Tyranny; and for one mifchief it prevented, ten thoufand evils, horrible and tremendous, fprung up in the place. Thenceforward every perfon's life and fortune depended on the vile breath of Informers. The Conftruction of words being arbitrary, and left to the decifion of the Judges, no man could write or open his Mouth, without being in danger of forfeiting his Head.

One was put to death, for inferting in his Hiftory, the praifes of *Brutus*; Another, for ftiling *Caffius* the *laft* of the *Romans*. *Caligula* valued himfelf for being a notable Dancer; To deny He excelled in that manly accomplifhment was High-Treafon. This Emperor advanced his Horfe *Incitatus* to the dignity of Conful; and, tho' Hiftory is filent, I don't queftion but it was a capital crime to fhow the leaft contempt for that High Officer of State. Suppofe then, any one had called the Prime Minifter a *ftupid animal*. The Emperor's Council might argue, that the malice of the Libel was aggravated by it's being true, and confequently more likely to excite the family of this illuftrious Magiftrate to acts of revenge. Such a profecution would appear ridiculous: Yet, if we may rely on Tra-

dition, there have been formerly Proconfuls in *America*, tho' of more malice, but hardly fuperior in underftanding to *Incitatus*, who would have thought themfelves *libelled*, to be called by their proper names.

Nero valued himfelf on his fine voice and fkill in mufick: a laudable ambition this! He performed in public and carried the prize. It was afterwards Refolved by all the Judges, as good Law, that whoever fhould infinuate the leaft doubt of *Nero's* Pre-eminence in THE NOBLE ART OF FIDLING, ought to be deemed a Traitor to the State.

By the help of Inferences and Innuendo's, Treafons multiplied in a prodigious manner. GRIEF was Treafon. A Lady of noble birth was put to death for bewailing the lofs of her murdered Son. Silence was declared an overt act to prove the treafonable purpofes of the heart. LOOKS were conftrued into Treafon. A ferene open afpect was an evidence that fhe Reafon was pleafed with the calamities that befel the Emperor. A fevere thoughtful countenance was urged againft the man that wore it, as a proof of his *plotting* againft the State. DREAMS were often made capital offences. A new fpecies of Informers went about *Rome*, infinuating themfelves in all companies to fifh out their Dreams, Which the holy Priefts, O! *nefarious wickednefs!* interpreted into High-Treafon. The *Romans* were fo terrified by this ftrange method of procefs, that, far from difcovering their Dreams, they durft not own that they flept. In this terrible fituation, when every one had fo much caufe to fear, even FEAR itfelf was made a crime. *Caligula* when he put his Brother to death, gave it as a reafon to the Senate, that the Youth was afraid of being murdered. To be eminent in any virtue, either civil or military, was the greateft crime a man could be guilty of. ------ *oh virtutes certiffimum exitium.*

Thefe were fome of the Effects of the Roman Law againft Libelling.

THOSE of the Britifh Kings who aimed at Defpotic Power, or the oppreffion of the Subject, conftantly encouraged profecutions for words.

Henry VII. a Prince mighty in politics, procured that Act to be paffed, whereby the jurifdiction of the Star-Chamber was confirmed and extended. Afterwards *Empfon* and *Dudley*, two voracious Dogs of prey, under the Protection of this High-Court, exercifed the moft mercilefs acts of oppreffion. The Subjects were terrified from uttering their griefs, while they faw the Thunder of the Star Chamber pointed at their Heads. This caution, however, could not prevent feveral dangerous tumults and infurrections. For when the Tongues of the People are reftrained, They commonly difcharge their refentments by a more *dangerous organ*, and break out into open acts of Violence.

During the Reign of *Henry* VIII. a high-fpirited Monarch, every light expreffion which happened to difpleafe him, was conftrued by his fouple Judges into a Libel, and fometimes extended to High-Treafon. When Queen *Mary* of Bloody Memory, afcended the Throne, the Parliament, in order to raife a Fence againft the violent Profecutions for Words, which had rendered the Lives, Liberties

---

sent of their legislature. He therefore applied to parliament, who passed an act for that purpose, limiting the number to be brought in and the time they were to continue. In like manner is his majesty restrained in every part of the empire. He possesses, indeed, the executive power of the laws in every state; but they are the laws of the particular state which he is to administer within that state, and not those of any one within the limits of another. Every state must judge for itself the number of armed men which they may safely trust among them, of whom they are to consist, and under what restrictions they shall be laid.

To render these proceedings still more criminal against our laws, instead of subjecting the military to the civil powers, his majesty has expressly made the civil subordinate to the military. But can his majesty thus put down all law under his feet? Can he erect a power superior to that which erected himself? He has done it indeed by force; but let him remember that force cannot give right.

That these are our grievances which we have thus laid before his majesty, with that freedom of language and sentiment which becomes a free people claiming their rights, as derived from the laws of nature, and not as the gift of their chief magistrate: Let those flatter who fear; it is not an American art. To give praise which is not due might be well from the venal, but would ill beseem those who are asserting the rights of human nature. They know, and will therefore say, that kings are the servants, not the proprietors of the people. Open your breast, sire, to liberal and expanded thought. Let not the name of George the third be a blot in the page of history. You are surrounded by British counsellors, but remember that they are parties. You have no ministers for American affairs, because you have none taken from among us, nor amenable to the laws on which they are to give you advice. It behoves you, therefore, to think and to act for yourself and your people. The great principles of right and wrong are legible to every reader; to pursue them requires not the aid of many counsellors. The whole art of government

consists in the art of being honest. Only aim to do your duty, and mankind will give you credit where you fail. No longer persevere in sacrificing the rights of one part of the empire to the inordinate desires of another; but deal out to all equal and impartial right. Let no act be passed by any one legislature which may infringe on the rights and liberties of another. This is the important post in which fortune has placed you, holding the balance of a great, if a well poised empire. This, sire, is the advice of your great American council, on the observance of which may perhaps depend your felicity and future fame, and the preservation of that harmony which alone can continue both to Great Britain and America the reciprocal advantages of their connection. It is neither our wish, nor our interest, to separate from her. We are willing, on our part, to sacrifice every thing which reason can ask to the restoration of that tranquility for which all must wish. On their part, let them be ready to establish union and a generous plan. Let them name their terms, but let them be just. Accept of every commercial preference it is in our power to give for such things as we can raise for their use, or they make for ours. But let them not think to exclude us from going to other markets to dispose of those commodities which they cannot use, or to supply those wants which they cannot supply. Still less let it be proposed that our properties within our own territories shall be taxed or regulated by any power on earth but our own. The God who gave us life gave us liberty at the same time; the hand of force may destroy, but cannot disjoin them. This, sire, is our last, our determined resolution; and that you will be pleased to interpose with that efficacy which your earnest endeavours may ensure to procure redress of these our great grievances, to quiet the minds of your subjects in British America, against any apprehensions of future encroachment, to establish fraternal love and harmony through the whole empire, and that these may continue to the latest ages of time, is the fervent prayer of all British America!

Thomas Jefferson's Statement on Rights of Colonists (1774)

A contemporary edition (1774) of Jefferson's pamphlet, A Summary View of the Rights of British America, described as "the boldest declaration of American rights that had yet been written." He voiced the noble sentiment which he later expressed in the Declaration of Independence: "The God who gave us Life, gave us Liberty at the same time.

Lent to The Freedom Train by the Library of Congress

Cambridge April 29: 1775

This may Certify that the bearer Mr Paul Revere is messenger to the Committee of Safety and that all dispatch and assistance be given him in all Instances, that the business of the Colony may be Facilitated ———

Jos Warren Chair

Paul Revere's Commission as Messenger

It was Joseph Warren who, on the evening of April 18, 1775, sent for Paul Revere and begged him to set off at once for Lexington to alert John Hancock and Samuel Adams to the fact that the British were on the march to seize them and the military stores at Concord. Although William Dawes, the other messenger, left Boston before Revere, it was Revere who first arrived to alert the two hunted patriots.

Several weeks after signing this Commission, General Warren was killed at Bunker Hill.

Lent to The Freedom Train by Dr. A. S. W. Rosenbach

The *American* CRISIS.

NUMBER I.

By the Author of COMMON SENSE.

THESE are the times that try men's souls: The summer soldier and the sunshine patriot will, in this crisis, shrink from the service of his country; but he that stands it NOW, deserves the love and thanks of man and woman. Tyranny, like hell, is not easily conquered; yet we have this consolation with us, that the harder the conflict, the more glorious the triumph. What we obtain too cheap, we esteem too lightly:---'Tis dearness only that gives every thing its value. Heaven knows how to set a proper price upon its goods; and it would be strange, indeed, if so celestial an article as FREEDOM should not be highly rated. Britain, with an army to enforce her tyranny, has declared, that she has a right (*not only to* TAX, but) "to " BIND *us in* ALL CASES WHATSOEVER," and if being *bound in that manner* is not slavery, then is there not such a thing as slavery upon earth. Even the expression is impious, for so unlimited a power can belong only to GOD.

WHETHER the Independence of the Continent was declared too soon, or delayed too long, I will not now enter into as an argument; my own simple opinion is, that had it been eight months earlier, it would have been much better. We did not make a proper use of last winter, neither could we, while we were in a dependent state. However, the fault, if it were one, was all our own; we have none to blame but ourselves*. But no great deal is lost yet; all that Howe has been doing for this month past is rather a ravage than a conquest, which the spirit of the Jersies a year ago would have quickly repulsed, and which time and a little resolution will soon recover.

I have as little superstition in me as any man living, but my

* "The present winter" (meaning the last) " is worth an " age if rightly employed, but if lost, or neglected, the whole " Continent will partake of the evil; and there is no punish- " ment that man does not deserve, be he who, or what, or " where he will, that may be the means of sacrificing a season " so precious and useful." COMMON SENSE.

Thomas Paine's The Crisis (1776)

This is a first printing of Number 1 of **The Crisis**, probably the most eloquent of all the pamphlets written during "The times that try men's souls." Composed during the bleak and discouraging winter of 1776 Paine lashed out at the "summer soldiers" and the "sunshine patriots."

Lent to The Freedom Train by Colonel Richard Gimbel

INTRODUCTION.

In the following Sheets, the Author hath studiously avoided every Thing which is personal among ourselves. Compliments as well as censure to Individuals make no Part thereof. The wise, and the worthy, need not the Triumph of a Pamphlet; and those whose Sentiments are injudicious, or unfriendly, will cease of themselves unless too much Pains are bestowed upon their Conversion.

The Cause of America is in a great Measure the Cause of all Mankind. Many Circumstances hath, and will arise, which are not local, but universal, and through which the Principles of all Lovers of Mankind are affected, and in the Event of which, their Affections are interested. The laying a Country desolate with Fire and Sword, declaring War against the natural Rights of all Mankind, and extirpating the Defenders thereof from the Face of the Earth, is the Concern of every Man to whom Nature hath given the Power of feeling; of which Class, regardless of Party Censure, is the

AUTHOR.

COMMON SENSE.

Of the Origin and Design of GOVERNMENT *in general, with concise Remarks on the* ENGLISH CONSTITUTION.

SOME writers have so confounded society with government, as to leave little or no distinction between them; whereas, they are not only different, but have different origins. Society is produced by our wants, and government by our wickedness; the former promotes our happiness *possitively* by uniting our affections, the latter *negatively* by restraining our vices. The one encourages intercourse, the other creates distinctions. The first is a patron, the last a punisher.

Society in every state is a blessing, but Government even in its best state is but a necessary evil; in its worst state an intolerable one: for when we suffer, or are exposed to the same miseries *by a Government*, which we might expect in a country *without Government*, our calamity is heightened by

B   reflect-

Thomas Paine's "Common Sense"

This is the first edition (published January 10, 1776) of Thomas Paine's celebrated pamphlet which was instrumental in swaying public opinion in favor of independence. Paine urged immediate independence not merely as a practical gesture but as the fulfillment of America's moral obligation to the world. In ringing terms he declared that the cause of liberty in America in that hour was the cause of liberty for all mankind. Paine was the first publicist to discover and articulate America's destiny and her mission in an unfree world.

The Body of
B. Franklin, Printer,
Like the Cover of an old Book,
Its Contents torn out,
And stript of its Lettering & Gilding,
Lies here, Food for Worms. —
But the Work shall not be lost;
For it will, as he believ'd, appear once more
In a new and more elegant Edition
Corrected and improved
By the Author. —

Given by B Franklin to Saml Morris
August 31 1776 ————

N.B. It is his own hand writing

Benjamin Franklin's Own Epitaph in His Own Hand

This copy of one of the most famous epitaphs in the English language was written out for Samuel Morris in Philadelphia and presented to him on August 31, 1776. Franklin, often termed "the first civilized American," found at least a few brief moments to indulge his sense of humor and whimsey.

Lent to The Freedom Train by Colonel Richard Gimbel

1776			York	Lawful
Augᵗ	By amᵗ broᵗ forward	£200 —	2676-7-9
Oct 9	By Cash from the Pay: master Genᵉ 1000 Doˡˡ			300 —
	York Curʸ 7ʳ redᵈ to Lawf	£200 — 50 —	297.6-7-9	150 —
	Amount of the money recᵈ from the Public in the Years 1775 & 6			3126-7-9
	By Ballᵃ due G. Washington & carrᵈ to accᵗ for 1777 *			599-19-11
			£ 3726 7 8

* This Ballᵈ arises from the expenditure
of my private purse. — From which (as
doth appear from the dates of the pub
lic debits against me) my outfit to
take the Command of the Army at Cam=
bridge — The Expences of the journey
thither — and disbursements for some
time afterwards, were borne — It being
money which I brought to, and recᵈ
at Philadelphia while there as a De=
legate to Congress, in May & June 1775

G. Washington

Washington's Revolutionary War Account Book in His Own Hand

When George Washington was chosen by the Continental Congress to be Commander-In-Chief of the American Armies, he stated that he would accept no payment but that he would keep an exact account of his expenses. So accurate were Washington's accounts (June 1776 to 1783) that a later audit showed, out of more than $160,000, a discrepancy of "89-90 of one dollar." The account contains a series of payments for espionage, although Washington kept secret the names of his agents. It also lists such items as "To Barber at Sundry times — 5 pounds 10 shillings." The double account columns were caused by the difference in the currency of the various colonies and "lawful" or coin currency.

Lent to The Freedom Train by the National Archives

(CONTINUED OPPOSITE SIDE)

Dr The United States .... in Acc

1776.			York			Lawful		
Sep.		To am.t bro.t forward ----	£	772.18.4		2757	12	4
Oct 2.		To Rich.d Peacock ----		2.11				
153..	10	To Capt.n Gibbs H.o Exp. 500 Do				150		
154	22	To Exp.e at Valentines						
		Mile Square --- 20 Do				6		
155	25.	To Mr Fleeson £4..6..0 Pa.y						
		deduct 25 p C.t ---- 17.2				3	8	10
156..	---	To Barber at sundry times		5.10				
157..	--	To Cash advanced Mons.r						
		Imbert French Enginr ----				6		
Dec.		To Household Expences						
159..	---	paid by Maj. Cary and						
		Bayler in Oct.r & part						
		of Nov.r while Capt.n						
		Gibbs was absent with						
		the Baggage --- p.r Acc.ts						
		settled --- viz 725½ Dol a 6/ ----				217	13	--
			£	780..19..4	+	3140	13	2
		York Cury. red.d to Lawful		195..4.10		585	14	6
		Expenditures of the						
		Years 1775 & 6 --- }			r	£3726.7.8		

No 104 £ 37..1..5
" 106   0..16..0
37..17.5 Penns.a Cury. Extended at Lawful } £7..11..5
         difference ----

Page 7 Short added --- £1..0..0
" 49 ---- Ditto ---- 0..1..0   1..1..0

                Deduct ----   6 10 5
                                        £ 3719 17 3

A Declaration by the Representatives of the UNITED STATES OF AMERICA, in General Congress assembled.

When in the course of human events it becomes necessary for one people to dissolve the political bands which have connected them with another, and to assume among the powers of the earth the separate and equal station to which the laws of nature & of nature's god entitle them, a decent respect to the opinions of mankind requires that they should declare the causes which impel them to the separation.

We hold these truths to be self-evident; that all men are created equal, that they are endowed by their creator with inherent & inalienable rights; that among these are life, liberty, & the pursuit of happiness; that to secure these rights, governments are instituted among men, deriving their just powers from the consent of the governed; that whenever any form of government becomes destructive of these ends, it is the right of the people to alter or to abolish it, & to institute new government, laying it's foundation on such principles & organising it's powers in such form, as to them shall seem most likely to effect their safety & happiness. prudence indeed will dictate that governments long established should not be changed for light & transient causes: and accordingly all experience hath shewn that mankind are more disposed to suffer while evils are sufferable, than to right themselves by abolishing the forms to which they are accustomed. but when a long train of abuses & usurpations [begun at a distinguished period, &] pursuing invariably the same object, evinces a design to reduce them under absolute Despotism, it is their right, it is their duty, to throw off such government & to provide new guards for their future security. such has been the patient sufferance of these colonies; & such is now the necessity which constrains them to alter their former systems of government. the history of the present king of Great Britain is a history of unremitting injuries and usurpations, among which appears no solitary fact to contradict the uniform tenor of the rest, but all have in direct object the establishment of an absolute tyranny over these states. to prove this, let facts be submitted to a candid world, for the truth of which we pledge a faith yet unsullied by falsehood.

Dr. Franklin's handwriting

Mr. Adams' hand writing

Jefferson's Rough Draft of the Declaration of Independence (June 11-28, 1776)

The original manuscript draft of the immortal statement of American liberties, by Thomas Jefferson, author of the Declaration of Independence, with verbal changes by Benjamin Franklin and John Adams noted thereon. This draft contains all changes and additions made from inception of document to its presentation to the Continental Congress. One of the most invaluable documents of American history. Note the marginal notations, "Franklin's handwriting" and "Adams' handwriting."

Lent to The Freedom Train by the Library of Congress

Nor have we been wanting in attentions to our British brethren. we have warned them from time to time of attempts by their legislature to extend a jurisdiction over [these our us states] we have reminded them of the circumstances of our emigration & settlement here, [no one of which could warrant so strange a pretension: that these were effected at the expence of our own blood & treasure, unassisted by the wealth or the strength of Great Britain: that in constituting indeed our several forms of government, we had adopted one common king, thereby laying a foundation for perpetual league & amity with them: but that submission to their

credited: and we have appealed to their native justice & magnanimity [as well as to the ties & we have conjured them by of our common kindred to disavow these usurpations which [were likely to] interrupt would inevitably our correspondence & connection. connection &   they too have been deaf to the voice of justice & of consanguinity. [& when occasions have been given them, by the regular course of We must therefore their laws, of removing from their councils the disturbers of our harmony, they have by their free election re-established them in power. at this very time too they are permitting their chief magistrate to send over not only soldiers of our common destroy us. blood, but Scotch & foreign mercenaries to invade & deluge us in blood. these facts have given the last stab to agonizing affection, and manly spirit bids us to renounce for ever these unfeeling brethren. we must endeavor to forget our former love for them, and to hold them as we hold the rest of mankind, enemies in war, in peace friends. we might have been a free & a great people together; but a communication of grandeur & of freedom it seems is below their dignity. be it so, since they & to glory. will have it. the road to happiness, is open to us too, we will tread it apart from them. and acquiesce in the necessity which denounces our de and hold them as we hold the rest of mankind enemies in war, in peace friends. eternal separation!

We therefore the representatives of the United States of America in General Congress assembled, do in the name & by authority of the good people of these [states,] appealing to the supreme judge of the world for the rectitude of our intentions colonies reject and renounce all allegiance & subjection to the kings of Great Britain & all others who may hereafter claim by, through, or under them; we utterly have dissolve & break off all political connection which may heretofore subsisted between us & the people or parliament of Great Britain; and finally we do assert and declare these colonies to be free and independant states, full and that as free & independant states they shall hereafter have power to levy war, conclude peace contract alliances, establish commerce, & to do all other acts and things which independant states may of right do. And for the support of this declaration we mutually pledge to each other our lives, our fortunes, & our sacred honour.

GLORIOUS NEWS.

PROVIDĒCE, October 25, 1781.

Three o'Clock, P. M.

THIS MOMENT an EXPRESS arrived at his Honour the Deputy-Governor's, from Col. Christopher Olney, Commandant on Rhode-Island, announcing the important Intelligence of the Surrender of Lord Cornwallis and his Army, an Account of which was printed This Morning at Newport, and is as follows, viz.

Newport, October 25, 1781.

YESTERDAY afternoon arrived in this Harbour Capt. Lovett, of the Schooner Adventure, from York-River, in Chesapeak-Bay (which he left the 20th Instant) and brought us the glorious News of the Surrender of Lord CORNWALLIS and his Army Prisoners of War to the allied Army, under the Command of our illustrious General, and the French Fleet, under the Command of his Excellency the Count de GRASSE.

A Cessation of Arms took Place on Thursday the 18th Instant, in Consequence of Proposals from Lord Cornwallis for a Capitulation. His Lordship proposed a Cessation of Twenty-four Hours, but Two only were granted by His Excellency General WASHINGTON. The Articles were completed the same Day, and the next Day the allied Army took Possession of York-Town.

By this glorious Conquest, NINE THOUSAND of the Enemy, including Seamen, fell into our Hands, with an immense Quantity of Warlike Stores, a forty Gun Ship, a Frigate, an armed Vessel, and about One Hundred Sail of Transports.

PRINTED BY EDWARD E. POWARS, in STATE-STREET.

"Glorious News" from Yorktown

The Momentous news of the surrender of Lord Cornwallis and his army, the virtual end of hostilities in the American Revolution, was carried by ship from Yorktown to Newport, Rhode Island, and thence was brought to Providence. The printer was in such haste to get the news to the people that he spelled Providence incorrectly in this original broadside.

Lent to The Freedom Train by Mrs. Frank Monaghan

Portsmouth New Hampshire Sept 2d
1782.

Your kind letter my dear Morris of the 13th
Ult. and the public one of the same date are
as welcome favors and as necessary to me
as fresh Air and the saving hand of Friendship to a drowning Man. — I know your
ability and am convinced your friendship
for our Country will manifest itself so
effectually that we may avail of the loss of
the Magnifique at Boston — I know it
has been proposed by some wise Heads to offer
the America as a present to replace that
ship. Are we in a condition to make
presents? If we were I should be against
offering to give a friend an empty Eggshell. —

The Honble
Gouverneur Morris Esqr Assistant Minister of Finance &c &c

Letter from John Paul Jones to Gouverneur Morris

The American Navy owes much of its heritage for heroism and victorious skill to the great John Paul Jones. This original letter to Gouverneur Morris is Jones' reply of September 2, 1782, to information that Congress had presented his ship "America" to the French Government in place of the foundered "Magnifique." With magnanimity he wrote, "As honorable peace is and always was my first wish, I can take no delight in the effusion of human blood, but if this war should continue, I wish to have the most active part in it."

(CONTINUED OPPOSITE SIDE)

Lent to The Freedom Train by the U. S. Naval Academy Museum

"you know me I find, since "you are sure I will rejoice at the present appearances of "Peace"— An honorable Peace is and always was my first wish. I can take no delight in the effusion of human Blood. but if this War should continue I wish to have the most active part in it.— With the highest sense of your kind attentions and good Opinion, and with the most earnest desire to deserve, by my conduct the delicate Praises of a Friend of your high worth and Public Spirit, I am, sincerely and affectionately

Your most obliged

John Paul Jones

Letter from John Paul Jones to Gouverneur Morris

(CONTINUED FROM OPPOSITE SIDE)

The engagement between Jones' "Bonhomme Richard" and the British "Serapis" is famous in world history. Competent historians have declared that the brilliant and unexpected victory was "wholly and solely due to the immovable courage of John Paul Jones." It was during this battle that Jones replied to the question of the British Captain Pearson, "Have you struck?", with his answer: "I have just begun to fight."

New York 14th July

My Dear General...

The events are uncertain, a Person amidst the most glaring prospects; may find at last nothing but a fantom, or only a Sight like in looking glace, which will never be a possession for enjoyment.

Drawing the tickets in the lottery of chance for so many Years, I am too well acquainted to depend upon probabilities where even certainties are so often doubtfull.

To put myself upon less precarious footing, I must contaract all possible accidents, that can befal me, and this by over sight am capable of.

Original Letter of Thaddeus Kosciuszko to General Nathanael Greene

Kosciuszko, known as "the George Washington of Poland," nobly served the cause of liberty during the American Revolution. During his lengthy sojourn in America he acquired a deep admiration for our institutions and freedoms. In this farewell letter before sailing for Europe in July 1786 he expressed his deep affection for the institutions and the people of the United States. Kosciuszko was a Colonel (stipend 60 dollars per month) in the Continental Army. His planning was largely responsible for our momentous victory at Saratoga. He also drew up the plans for the fortification at West Point.

Lent to The Freedom Train by the Museum of the Polish Roman Catholic Union of America, Chicago

W

E the People of the States of New-Hampſhire, Maſſachuſetts, Rhode-Iſland and Providence Plan-tations, Connecticut, New-York, New-Jerſey, Penn-ſylvania, Delaware, Maryland, Virginia, North-Caro-lina, South-Carolina, and Georgia, do ordain, declare and eſtabliſh the following Conſtitution for the Govern-ment of Ourſelves and our Poſterity.

ARTICLE I.

The ſtile of this Government ſhall be, " The United States of America."

II.

The Government ſhall conſiſt of ſupreme legiſlative, executive and judicial powers.

III.

The legiſlative power ſhall be veſted in a Congreſs, to conſiſt of two ſeparate and diſtinct bodies of men, a Houſe of Repreſentatives, and a Senate ; ~~each of which ſhall, in all caſes, have a negative on the other. The Legiſlature ſhall meet on the firſt Monday in December in every year.~~

IV.

Sect. 1. The Members of the Houſe of Repreſentatives ſhall be choſen eve-ry ſecond year, by the people of the ſeveral States comprehended within this Union. The qualifications of the electors ſhall be the ſame, from time to time, as thoſe of the electors in the ſeveral States, of the moſt numerous branch of their own legiſlatures.

Sect. 2. Every Member of the Houſe of Repreſentatives ſhall be of the age of twenty-five years at leaſt ; ſhall have been a citizen of the United States for at leaſt ~~three~~ years before his election ; and ſhall be, at the time of his e-lection, *an inhabitant* ~~a reſident~~ of the State in which he ſhall be choſen

Sect. 3. The Houſe of Repreſentatives ſhall, at its firſt formation, and until the number of citizens and inhabitants ſhall be taken in the manner herein af-ter deſcribed, conſiſt of ſixty-five Members, of whom three ſhall be choſen in New-Hampſhire, eight in Maſſachuſetts, one in Rhode-Iſland and Providence Plantations, five in Connecticut, ſix in New-York, four in New-Jerſey, eight in Pennſylvania, one in Delaware, ſix in Maryland, ten in Virginia, five in North-Carolina, five in South-Carolina, and three in Georgia.

Sect. 4. As the proportions of numbers in the different States will alter from time to time; as ſome of the States may hereafter be divided; as others may be enlarged by addition of territory ; as two or more States may be united; as new States will be erected within the limits of the United States, the Legiſla-ture ſhall, in each of theſe caſes, regulate the number of repreſentatives by the number of inhabitants, according to the ~~proportion herein after~~ ~~mentioned~~ rate of one for every forty thouſand. *Provided that every State ſhall have at least one repreſentative.*

Sect. 5. All bills for raiſing or appropriating money, and for fixing the ſala-ries of the officers of government, ſhall originate in the Houſe of Repreſenta-tives, and ſhall not be altered or amended by the Senate. No money ſhall be drawn from the public Treaſury, but in purſuance of appropriations that ſhall originate in the Houſe of Repreſentatives.

Sect. 6. The Houſe of Repreſentatives ſhall have the ſole power of impeach-ment. It ſhall chooſe its Speaker and other officers.

Sect. 7. Vacancies in the Houſe of Repreſentatives ſhall be ſupplied by writs of election from the executive authority of the State, in the repreſentation from which they ſhall happen. **V.**

[Handwritten margin note:] * The Legiſlature ſhall meet at least once in every year, and that meeting ſhall be on the firſt Monday in December unless a different day ſhall be appointed by law.

[Handwritten margin note:] a State to

[Handwritten margin note:] ſtruck out

Washington's Own Copy of the Constitution (1787)

As President of the Constitutional Convention, Washington was an important figure in forging the basic frame-work of our government. This printed draft of the Constitution as it was reported to the Committee on Detail in August, 1787, was Washington's personal copy. It shows corrections made in his large, firm handwriting. At this stage of the drafting of the Constitution, the separate sovereignties of the States had not yet been merged, in the thinking of the delegates, into the United States, as indicated by the opening sentence: "We the People of the States of New-Hampshire, Massachusetts, . . . etc."

Lent to The Freedom Train by the National Archives

An ORDINANCE for the GOVERNMENT of the TERRITORY of the UNITED STATES, North-West of the RIVER OHIO.

BE IT ORDAINED by the United States in Congress assembled, That the said territory, for the purposes of temporary government, be one district; subject, however, to be divided into two districts, as future circumstances may, in the opinion of Congress, make it expedient.

Be it ordained by the authority aforesaid, That the estates both of resident and non-resident proprietors in the said territory, dying intestate, shall descend to, and be distributed among their children, and the descendants of a deceased child in equal parts; the descendants of a deceased child or grand-child, to take the share of their deceased parent in equal parts among them: And where there shall be no children or descendants, then in equal parts to the next of kin, in equal degree; and among collaterals, the children of a deceased brother or sister of the intestate, shall have in equal parts among them their deceased parents share; and there shall in no case be a distinction between kindred of the whole and half blood; saving in all cases to the widow of the intestate, her third part of the real estate for life, and one third part of the personal estate; and this law relative to descents and dower, shall remain in full force until altered by the legislature of the district. ———— And until the governor and judges shall adopt laws as herein after mentioned, estates in the said territory may be devised or bequeathed by wills in writing, signed and sealed by him or her, in whom the estate may be, (being of full age) and attested by three witnesses; ——— and real estates may be conveyed by lease and release, or bargain and sale, signed, sealed, and delivered by the person being of full age, in whom the estate may be, and attested by two witnesses, provided such wills be duly proved, and such conveyances be acknowledged, or the execution thereof duly proved, and be recorded within one year after proper magistrates, courts, and registers shall be appointed for that purpose; and personal property may be transferred by delivery, saving, however, to the French and Canadian inhabitants, and other settlers of the Kaskaskies, Saint Vincent's, and the neighbouring villages, who have heretofore professed themselves citizens of Virginia, their laws and customs now in force among them, relative to the descent and conveyance of property.

Be it ordained by the authority aforesaid, That there shall be appointed from time to time, by Congress, a governor, whose commission shall continue in force for the term of three years, unless sooner revoked by Congress; he shall reside in the district, and have a freehold estate therein, in one thousand acres of land, while in the exercise of his office.

There shall be appointed from time to time, by Congress, a secretary, whose commission shall continue in force for four years, unless sooner revoked, he shall reside in the district, and have a freehold estate therein, in five hundred acres of land, while in the exercise of his office; it shall be his duty to keep and preserve the acts and laws passed by the legislature, and the public records of the district, and the proceedings of the governor in his executive department; and transmit authentic copies of such acts and proceedings, every six months, to the secretary of Congress: There shall also be appointed a court to consist of three judges, any two of whom to form a court, who shall have a common law jurisdiction, and reside in the district, and have each therein a freehold estate in five hundred acres of land, while in the exercise of their offices; and their commissions shall continue in force during good behaviour.

The governor and judges, or a majority of them, shall adopt and publish in the district, such laws of the original states, criminal and civil, as may be necessary, and best suited to the circumstances of the district, and report them to Congress, from time to time, which laws shall be in force in the district until the organization of the general assembly therein, unless disapproved of by Congress; but afterwards the legislature shall have authority to alter them as they shall think fit.

The governor for the time being, shall be commander in chief of the militia, appoint and commission all officers in the same, below the rank of general officers; all general officers shall be appointed and commissioned by Congress.

Previous to the organization of the general assembly, the governor shall appoint such magistrates and other civil officers, in each county or township, as he shall find necessary for the preservation of the peace and good order in the same: After the general assembly shall be organized, the powers and duties of magistrates and other civil officers shall be regulated and defined by the said assembly; but all magistrates and other civil officers, not herein otherwise directed, shall, during the continuance of this temporary government, be appointed by the governor.

For the prevention of crimes and injuries, the laws to be adopted or made shall have force in all parts of the district, and for the execution of process, criminal and civil, the governor shall make proper divisions thereof——and he shall proceed from time to time, as circumstances may require, to lay out the parts of the district in which the Indian titles shall have been extinguished, into counties and townships, subject, however, to such alterations as may thereafter be made by the legislature.

So soon as there shall be five thousand free male inhabitants, of full age, in the district, upon giving proof thereof to the governor, they shall receive authority, with time and place, to elect representatives from their counties or townships, to represent them in the general assembly; provided that for every five hundred free male inhabitants there shall be one representative, and so on progressively with the number of free male inhabitants, shall the right of representation increase, until the number of representatives shall amount to twenty-five, after which the number and proportion of representatives shall be regulated by the legislature; provided that no person be eligible or qualified to act as a representative, unless he shall have been a citizen of one of the United States three years and be a resident in the district, or unless he shall have resided in the district three years, and in either case shall likewise hold in his own right, in fee simple, two hundred acres of land within the same:——Provided also, that a freehold in fifty acres of land in the district, having been a citizen of one of the states, and being resident in the district; or the like freehold and two years residence in the district shall be necessary to qualify a man as an elector of a representative.

The representatives thus elected, shall serve for the term of two years, and in case of the death of a representative, or removal from office, the governor shall issue a writ to the county or township for which he was a member, to elect another in his stead, to serve for the residue of the term.

The general assembly, or legislature, shall consist of the governor, legislative council, and a house of representatives. The legislative council shall consist of five members, to continue in office five years, unless sooner removed by Congress, any three of whom to be a quorum, and the members of the council shall be nominated and appointed in the following manner, to wit: As soon as representatives shall be elected, the governor shall appoint a time and place for them to meet together, and, when met, they shall nominate ten persons, residents in the district, and each possessed of a freehold in five hundred acres of land, and return their names to Congress; five of whom Congress shall appoint and commission to serve as aforesaid; and whenever a vacancy shall happen in the council, by death or removal from office, the house of representatives shall nominate two persons, qualified as aforesaid, for each vacancy, and return their names to Congress; one of whom Congress shall appoint and commission for the residue of the term; and every five years, four months at least before the expiration of the time of service of the members of council, the said house shall nominate ten persons, qualified as aforesaid, and return their names to Congress, five of whom Congress shall appoint and commission to serve as members of the council five years, unless sooner removed. And the governor, legislative council, and house of re-

---

it be regulated by law, the amendment which declares that Congress shall make no law to abridge the freedom of the press, which freedom however may be regulated by law, is the grossest absurdity, that ever was conceived by the human mind.

That by the words " freedom of the press" is meant a total exemption of the press from legislative control, will further appear, from the following cases, in which it is manifest, that the word freedom is used with this signification and no other.

It is obvious in itself, and it is admitted by all men, that freedom of speech, means the power uncontrolled by law, of speaking either truth or falsehood at the discretion of the individual, provided no other *individual* be injured. This power is, *as yet*, in its full extent in the United States. A man may say every thing which his passion can suggest, he may employ all his time and all his talents, if he is wicked enough to do so, in *speaking* against the government matters that are false, scandalous, and malicious, but he is admitted by the majority of Congress to be sheltered by the article in question, which forbids a law abridging the freedom of speech. If then freedom of speech means, in the construction of the constitution, the

the privilege of speaking *any thing* without control, the words freedom of the press, which form a part of the same sentence, mean the privilege of printing *any thing* without control.

Happily for mankind, the word " freedom" begins now to be applied to religion also. In the United States it is applied in its fullest force, and religious freedom is completely understood to mean the power uncontrolled by law of professing and publishing any opinions on religious topics, which any individual may choose to profess or publish, and of supporting those opinions by any statements he may think proper to make. The fool may not only say in his heart, there is no God, but he may announce if he pleases his atheism to the world. He may endeavor to corrupt mankind, not only by opinions that are erroneous, but by facts which are false. Still however he will be safe, because he lives in a country where religious freedom is established. If then freedom of religion, will not permit a man to be punished, for publishing any opinions on religious topics, and supporting those opinions by false facts, surely freedom of the press, which is the medium of all publications, will not permit a man to be punished, for publishing any opinion on

D3   any

An Essay on the Liberty of the Press by George Hay (1799)

An influential book which argued in legal terms the need for freeing the press from any outside influence. In 1798 a "Sedition Act" was designed to silence derogatory criticism of the Government and of Public Officials. It was vigorously enforced and several editors were imprisoned or ruined by heavy fines. One of the best protests to the "Sedition Act" was written by George Hay an attorney, who was later appointed as an U. S. attorney by President Thomas Jefferson. Hay stated that freedom of the press means the exemption of the press from legislative control.

To the Hebrew Congregation in Newport
Rhode Island.

Gentlemen.

While I receive, with much satisfaction, your Address replete with expressions of affection and esteem; I rejoice in the opportunity of assuring you, that I shall always retain a grateful remembrance of the cordial welcome I experienced in my visit to Newport, from all classes of Citizens.

The reflection on the days of difficulty and danger which are past is rendered the more sweet, from a consciousness that they are succeeded by days of uncommon prosperity and security. If we have wisdom to make the best use of the advantages with which we are now favored, we cannot fail, under the just administration of a good Government, to become a great and a happy people.

The Citizens of the United States of America have a right to applaud themselves for having given to mankind examples of an enlarged and liberal policy: a policy worthy of imitation. All possess alike liberty of conscience and immunities of citizenship. It is now no more that toleration is spoken of, as if it was by the indulgence of one class of people, that another enjoyed the exercise of their inherent natural rights. For happily the

the Government of the United States, which gives to bigotry no sanction, to persecution no assistance, requires only that they who live under its protection, should demean themselves as good citizens, in giving it on all occasions their effectual support.

It would be inconsistent with the frankness of my character not to avow that I am pleased with your favorable opinion of my administration, and fervent wishes for my felicity. May the children of the Stock of Abraham, who dwell in this land, continue to merit and enjoy the good will of the other Inhabitants; while every one shall sit in safety under his own vine and figtree, and there shall be none to make him afraid. May the father of all mercies scatter light and not darkness in our paths, and make us all in our several vocations useful here, and in his own due time and way everlastingly happy.

G⁰ Washington

DISCOURS

DU COMTE DE MIRABEAU,

Dans la séance de ce matin 11 Juin.

SUR LA MORT

DE BENJAMIN FRANKLIN.

MESSIEURS,

FRANKLIN est mort.... Il est retourné au sein de la Divinité, le génie qui affranchit l'Amérique et versa sur l'Europe des torrens de lumière.

Le Sage que deux mondes reclament, l'homme que se disputent l'histoire des sciences et l'histoire des empires, tenoit sans doute un rang élevé dans l'espèce humaine.

The Tribute of France to the Memory of Dr. Franklin (1790)

This is the first separate pamphlet printing of the celebrated speech of Mirabeau, the greatest orator of the French Revolution, rendering tribute in the National Convention to the memory of Dr. Benjamin Franklin. Mirabeau paid homage to "one of the greatest men who have ever been engaged in the service of philosophy and liberty . . . a mighty genius, who, to the advantage of mankind, compassing in his mind the heavens and the earth, was able to restrain alike thunderbolts and tyrants . . . the philosopher who has most contributed to the extension of the rights of man over the whole earth." The French National Convention decreed three days of mourning in his memory.

Lent to The Freedom Train by the Sterling Memorial Library, Yale University

Congreſs of the United States :

AT THE THIRD SESSION,

Begun and held at the city of Philadelphia, on
Monday the ſixth of December, one thouſand ſeven hundred and ninety.

RESOLVED *by the* SENATE *and* HOUSE *of* REPRESENTATIVES
of the United States of America in Congreſs aſſembled, That the
Preſident of the United States be requeſted to cauſe to be communicated to the National Aſſembly of France the peculiar ſenſibility of
Congreſs to the tribute paid to the memory of Benjamin Franklin,
by the enlightened and free repreſentatives of a great nation, in their
decree of the eleventh of June, one thouſand ſeven hundred and
ninety.

FREDERICK AUGUSTUS MUHLENBERG,
Speaker of the Houſe of Repreſentatives.

JOHN ADAMS, *Vice-Preſident of the United States,*
and Preſident of the Senate.

APPROVED, March the ſecond, 1791.

GEORGE WASHINGTON, *Preſident of the United States.*

The Thanks of the Congress of the United States to the French Nation (1791)

An original broadside in which the Congress of the United States officially thanked "the enlightened and
free representatives of a great nation" for the tribute paid to the memory of Dr. Franklin by the National
Assembly. By this action Congress itself rendered indirect and belated tribute to one of the greatest of all
Americans. It was a matter of embarrassment to many Americans of the time that, although the French Government had decreed official mourning for Franklin, The U. S. Congress had not.

Lent to The Freedom Train by Mr. Frederic R. Kirkland

As this Address, Fellow citizens, will be the last I shall ever make to you, and as some of the Gazettes of the United States have teemed with all the Invective that disappointment, ignorance of facts, and malicious falsehoods could invent, to misrepresent my politics & affections;—to wound my reputation and feelings;—and to weaken, if not entirely to destroy the confidence you had been pleased to repose in me; it might be expected at the parting scene of my public life that I should take some notice of such virulent abuse—But, as heretofore, I shall pass them over in utter silence; never having myself, nor by any other with my participation or knowledge, written or published a scrap in answer to any of them.—My politicks have been uncon-cealed—plain and direct.—They will be found (so far as they relate to the Belligerent Powers) in the Proclamation of the 22 of April 1793; which, having met your approbation, and the confirmation of Congress, I have uniformly & steadily adhered to them—uninfluenced by, and regardless of, the complaints & attempts of any of those or their partizans Powers to change them.—

President Washington's Farewell Address (1796)

Original manuscript in Washington's handwriting of one of the most famous documents of American history. In the management of government he urged the preservation of public credit. He did not, however, advocate unwise economies, for he noted "timely disbursements to prepare for danger frequently prevent much greater disbursements to repel it."

(CONTINUED OPPOSITE SIDE)

Lent to The Freedom Train by the New York State Library, Albany

been blessed amidst the tumults which have
and involved in all the horrors of War
harrassed other countries. — I leave you with
undefiled hands — an uncorrupted heart —
and with ardent vows to heaven for the Welfare & happiness of that country in which I
and my forefathers to the third or fourth
Progenitor
Ancestry drew our first breath. —

G: Washington

President Washington's Farewell Address (1796)

Washington stated, "The name American, which belongs to you in your national capacity, must always exalt the just pride of Patriotism . . . " This, the original manuscript, is entirely in Washington's handwriting. Washington later showed it to Alexander Hamilton with the request that he "redress" it. Using his own draft and the combined suggestions of Alexander Hamilton and John Jay, Washington prepared the version which was ultimately released to the American people.

O say can you see, ~~through~~ by the dawn's early light,
What so proudly we hail'd at the twilight's last gleaming,
Whose broad stripes & bright stars through the perilous fight
O'er the ramparts we watch'd, were so gallantly streaming?
And the rocket's red glare, the bomb bursting in air,
Gave proof through the night that our flag was still there,
O say does that star spangled banner yet wave
O'er the land of the free & the home of the brave?

On the shore dimly seen through the mists of the deep,
Where the foe's haughty host in dread silence reposes,
What is that which the breeze, o'er the towering steep,
As it fitfully blows, half conceals, half discloses?
Now it catches the gleam of the morning's first beam,
In full glory reflected now shines in the stream,
'Tis the star-spangled banner — O long may it wave
O'er the land of the free & the home of the brave!

And where is that band who so vauntingly swore,
That the havoc of war & the battle's confusion
A home & a Country should leave us no more?
— ~~Their blood~~
Their blood has wash'd out their foul footstep's pollution.
No refuge could save the hireling & slave
From the terror of flight or the gloom of the grave,
And the star-spangled banner in triumph doth wave
O'er the land of the free & the home of the brave.

O thus be it ever when freemen shall stand
Between their lov'd home & the war's desolation!
Blest with vict'ry & peace may the heav'n rescued land
Praise the power that hath made & preserv'd us a nation!
Then conquer we must, when our cause it is just,
And this be our motto — "In God is our trust,"
And the star-spangled banner in triumph shall wave
O'er the land of the free & the home of the brave. —

Original Manuscript of "The Star Spangled Banner" (September, 1814)

Upon his release from the British ship from which he witnessed the unsuccessful attack against Fort McHenry (War of 1812) Francis Scott Key returned to his Baltimore hotel and wrote some fragmentary notes in the form of a song with the metre of a popular tune of the day, "Anacreon in Heaven." The next morning it was sent to the printer to be struck off in handbills. This manuscript, in the author's handwriting, is the original that was used by the printer.

Lent to The Freedom Train by the Walters Art Gallery, Baltimore

Remarks and Occurrences on board U. S. Frigate Constitution Charles Stewart Esqr. Commr. on a cruise
Wednesday February 8. 1815.

First part fresh breezes with squally and cloudy.

Middle part like weather.

Latter part baffling variable winds. At 7h. 30m. A. M. spoke and boarded the barque Julia under Hamburg colours from Cork bound to Lisbon out 15 days, informed us that the news at Cork when they left was, that peace had been signed at Ghent between the British and American Commissioners. At meridian discovered a sail on the larboard bow, hauled up and made sail in chase.

Course	Distance	Departure	Diff Lat.	Lat by Acct	Lat Obs	Longe in	Longe by Chronometer	Longe by Observation	Variation	Wounded	Killed	Sick	died
			0. 30. N.		42. 26. N.								

Logbook of the U. S. Frigate "Constitution" (1815)
RELATES NEWS OF END OF WAR OF 1812

Best-beloved ship in the U. S. Navy, the Frigate "Constitution," or "Old Ironsides," as she is known, symbolizes the indomitable strength and spirit of the Navy and her fighting men. Launched in 1797, the "Constitution" is still afloat. She especially distinguished herself in the War of 1812. This original log, open at the entry of February 8, 1815, records the receipt of the news that the war had ended and the peace treaty been signed in Ghent in December 1814. Meanwhile, not knowing that peace had been made, the "Constitution" had been in several engagements and had captured some ships as prizes.

The Log states, in part: " - - - spoke and boarded the barque Julia under Hamburg colours from Cork bound to Lisbon out 15 days, informed us that the news at Cork when they left was, that peace had been signed at Ghent between the British and American Commissioners. At meridian discovered a sail on the larboard bow, hauled up and made sail in chase."

Thus the "Constitution" heard unconfirmed reports of the war's end - - - and proceeded with its maritime activities.

By the President of the United States of America:

A Proclamation.

Whereas, on the twenty-second day of September, in the year of our Lord one thousand eight hundred and sixty-two, a proclamation was issued by the President of the United States, containing, among other things, the following, to wit:

"That on the first day of January, in the "year of our Lord one thousand eight hundred "and sixty-three, all persons held as slaves within "any State or designated part of a State, the people "whereof shall then be in rebellion against the "United States, shall be then, thenceforward, and "forever free; and the Executive Government of the "United States, including the military and naval "authority thereof, will recognize and maintain "the freedom of such persons, and will do no act "or acts to repress such persons, or any of them, "in any efforts they may make for their actual "freedom.

"That the Executive will, on the first day

The Emancipation Proclamation

Lincoln, the "Great Emancipator," embodied a growing American abhorrence of slavery that was climaxed by the Civil War. Although a military measure, the Emancipation Proclamation, issued on January 1, 1863, freed the slaves in most of the territory in arms against the Federal Government, and foreshadowed the abolition of slavery itself. The first and signature pages of the official proclamation bearing Lincoln's signature and the seal of the United States are shown.

Lent to The Freedom Train by the National Archives

one thousand eight hundred
and sixty three, and of the
Independence of the United
States of America the eighty-
seventh.

Abraham Lincoln

By the President:

William H. Seward
Secretary of State.

Four score and seven years ago our fathers brought forth, upon this continent, a new nation, conceived in Liberty, and dedicated to the proposition that all men are created equal.

Now we are engaged in a great civil war, testing whether that nation, or any nation, so conceived, and so dedicated, can long endure. We are met here on a great battlefield of that war. We have come to dedicate a portion of it, as a final resting place for those who here gave their lives that that nation might live. It is altogether fitting and proper that we should do this.

But in a larger sense we can not dedicate— we can not consecrate— we can not hallow this ground. The brave men, living and dead, who struggled here, have consecrated it far above our poor power to add or detract. The world will little note, nor long remember, what we say here, but can never forget what they did here. It is for us, the living, rather to be dedicated here to the unfinished work which they have, thus far, so nobly carried on. It is rather

---

Abraham Lincoln's Gettysburg Address (November 19, 1863)

This is the original manuscript in Lincoln's handwriting, which he held in his hand while making his classic address at Gettysburg. He had made three copies of the speech before coming to Gettysburg, none of which contained his immortal words "under God' after the words "this nation" which he added in his actual address. It is not true that he wrote the speech on the back of an old envelope on the train on his way to Gettysburg. This speech, which has become a part of the universal language of liberty and human dignity, was not originally scheduled by the Committee. Lincoln was asked to speak only as a matter of protocol and politeness, and to make a few appropriate remarks. His address has long since been enshrined in the pages of history.

Lent to The Freedom Train by the Library of Congress

for us to be here dedicated to the great
task remaining before us— that from these
honored dead we take increased devotion
to the cause for which they here gave
the last full measure of devotion— that
we here highly resolve that these dead
shall not have died in vain; that this
nation shall have a new birth of freedom;
and that this government of the people, by
the people, for the people, shall not perish
from the earth.

Powhatan Co: 24 Aug '65

Gentlemen

I have delayed for some days, replying to your letter of the 5 Inst: informing one of my election by the Board of Trustees, to the Presidency of Washington College—, from a desire to give the subject due consideration. Fully impressed with the responsibilities of the office, I have feared that I should be unable to discharge its duties, to the satisfaction of the Trustees, or to the benefit of the Country. The proper education, of youth requires not only great ability, but I fear more strength than I now possess, for I do not feel able to undergo the labour of conducting classes in regular courses of instruction. I could not therefore undertake more than the general administration & supervision of the Institution. There is another subject which has caused me serious reflection, & is I think worthy of the consideration of the Board. Being excluded from the terms of amnesty in the proclamation of the President of the U.S. of the 29 May last, & an object of censure to a portion of the Country, I have thought it probable that my occupation of the position of President, might draw upon the College a feeling of hostility; & I should therefore cause injury to an Institution, which it would be my highest desire to advance. I think it the duty of every citizen

in the present Condition of the County, to do all in
his power to aid in the restoration of peace & harmony,
& in no way to oppose the policy of the State or Fed Governments, directed to that object. It is particularly
incumbent on those charged with the instruction
of the young, to set them an example of submission
to authority, & I could not consent to be the cause of
animadversion upon the College.

Should you however take a different view, &
think that my services in the position tendered
me by the Board will be advantageous to the
College & Country, I will yield to your judgment
& accept it. Otherwise I must most respectfully
decline the office.

Begging you to express to the trustees of the
College my heartfelt gratitude for the honour
conferred upon me, & requesting you to accept
my cordial thanks for the kind manner in which
you have communicated its decision,
I am Gentn with great respect
your most obt Sevt

R E Lee

Messrs John W. Brockenbrough Rector
S. McD Reid . Alfred Leyburn
Horatio Thompson D.D. Bolivar Christian
I. I. Kirkpatrick
Committee

National Woman Suffrage Association.

President, SUSAN B. ANTHONY,
Rochester, N.Y.

Ch'n Ex. Com. MATILDA JOSLYN GAGE,
Fayetteville, N.Y.

Cor. Sec'y, JANE GRAHAM JONES,
910 Prairie Ave., Chicago, Ill.

For. Cor. Sec'y, LAURA CURTIS BULLARD,
85 East Thirty-ninth St., New York.

Rec. Sec'y, MARY F. DAVIS,
Orange, New Jersey.

Treasurer, ELLEN C. SARGENT,
Washington, D.C.

1873.

To the Honorable Senate and House of Representatives in Congress assembled:

We the undersigned, citizens of the United States, but deprived of some of the privileges and immunities of citizens, among which is the right to vote, beg leave to submit the following Resolution:—

Resolved; That we, the officers and members of the National Woman Suffrage Association, in Convention assembled; Respectfully ask Congress to enact appropriate legislation during its present session to protect women citizens in the several States of this Union, in their right to vote.

Susan B. Anthony Pr.

Matilda Joslyn Gage Ch. Ex. Com.

Elizabeth Cady Stanton

Petition of the National Women's Suffrage Association to Congress (1873)

From the beginning of the Republic, American women sought to obtain civil rights, but it was 1848 before an organized movement for such rights began. Elizabeth Cady Stanton and Susan B. Anthony were two of the leaders who in 1869 formed the National Women's Suffrage Association. They signed this 1873 petition of the Association to Congress, which asks for legislation to protect women in their right to vote in the several States.

Lent to The Freedom Train by the National Archives

Sixty-sixth Congress of the United States of America;

At the First Session,

Begun and held at the City of Washington on Monday, the nineteenth day of May,
one thousand nine hundred and nineteen.

JOINT RESOLUTION

Proposing an amendment to the Constitution extending the right of suffrage
to women.

---

*Resolved by the Senate and House of Representatives of the United States
of America in Congress assembled (two-thirds of each House concurring therein),*
That the following article is proposed as an amendment to the Constitution,
which shall be valid to all intents and purposes as part of the Constitution when
ratified by the legislatures of three-fourths of the several States.

"ARTICLE ————.

"The right of citizens of the United States to vote shall not be denied or
abridged by the United States or by any State on account of sex.

"Congress shall have power to enforce this article by appropriate
legislation."

F. H. Gillett

Speaker of the House of Representatives.

Thos. R. Marshall

Vice President of the United States and
President of the Senate.

The Nineteenth Amendment

"The right of citizens of the United States to vote shall not be denied or abridged by the United States or
by any State on account of sex."

Women's long struggle for the right to vote was crowned with success when the nineteenth amendment to
the Constitution was adopted on August 26, 1920. The original amendment, in the usual form of a joint resolution to Congress, dated May 18, 1919, proposing the extension of the right of suffrage to women, is displayed.

Lent to The Freedom Train by the National Archives

PROCLAMATION!

To the Inhabitants of Guam:

In issuing this decree the Government desires and earnestly invokes Divine blessing and guidance in its official action and in the daily pursuits and occupations of the citizens of Guam.

By the cession of the Isle of Guam to the United States of America, all of the authority, power and responsibilities of sovereignty were transferred to this Government, and in transforming and organizing the new political power the surest and speediest route to success, prosperity and happiness for the inhabitants of this island is by benevolent assimilation to the fundamental principles that constitute the basis of Free American Government.

Honest labor with just compensation, dignified by faithful consideration of the mutual interests and welfare of all persons concerned, should insure prosperity to this community; whereas, the existing labor-degrading system of human bondage and unjust, indefinite servitude or Peonage, permitted during the late Spanish control in this island, is, in fact, a system of Slavery, and as such, is subversive of good government, is an obstacle to progressive civilization, a menace to popular liberty, and a violation of the sacred privileges guaranteed by the Constitution of the United States.

Now, therefore, by virtue of the authority vested in me by his Excellency, the President of the United States, I, Richard P. Leary, Captain, United States Navy, Governor of the Isle of Guam, do hereby announce and publicly proclaim absolute prohibition and total abolition of Human Slavery or Peonage in the Isle of Guam on and after the Twenty-second day of February, A. D. 1900, and all persons are hereby commanded to comply with the requirements of this proclamation.

In witness whereof, I have hereunto set my hand and have caused the seal of the United States Naval Station, Isle of Guam, to be affixed.

Done at Agana, Isle of Guam, this First day of January, in the year of our Lord, One Thousand Nine Hundred, and of the Independence of the United States of America, the One Hundred and Twenty-fourth.

RICHARD P. LEARY, U. S. N.,
GOVERNOR.

Naval Governor of the Isle of Guam, Abolishing Slavery and Peonage

Our policy has been to extend as rapidly as possible the privileges of free, democratic government to people under our jurisdiction. Accordingly, the United States, when it acquired Guam after the Spanish-American War, as a first step abolished slavery and peonage in the Isle. The official printed proclamation of February 22, 1900, of Richard P. Leary, the naval governor of the island, is displayed.

Lent to The Freedom Train by the National Archives

January 22, 1907.

My dear Mr. Secretary:

In reference to Magoon's two letters of the 13th and 16th, which are returned herewith, I need hardly add to what I said this morning.   There can be no talk of a protectorate by us.   Our business is to establish peace and order on a satisfactory basis, start the new government, and then leave the Island; the Cuban Government taking the reins into its own hands; tho of course it might be advisable for some little time that some of our troops should stay in the Islands to steady things.   I will not even consider the plan of a protectorate, or any plan which would imply our breaking our explicit promise because of which we were able to prevent a war of devastation last fall.   The good faith of the United States is a mighty valuable asset and must not be impaired.

Sincerely yours,

Theodore Roosevelt

Hon. Wm. H. Taft,
    Secretary of War.

Original Letter of President Theodore Roosevelt to Secretary of War William Howard Taft in Regard to Keeping Our Promise to Get Out of Cuba

Keeping faith with countries and peoples over whom the United States has acquired control has been a cardinal principle of American policy. After the Spanish-American War and in 1907, when we were again in Cuba, many urged that we annex the island. President Theodore Roosevelt emphatically rejected such proposals, as his signed letter of January 22, 1907, to Secretary of War William Howard Taft shows.

Lent to The Freedom Train by the National Archives

I call upon all the loyal citizens engaged in production for defense to give precedence to the needs of the nation to the end that a system of government that makes private enterprise possible may survive.

I call upon all our loyal workmen as well as employers to merge their lesser differences in the larger effort to insure the survival of the only kind of government which recognizes the rights of labor or of capital.

I call upon loyal state and local leaders and officials to cooperate with the civilian defense agencies of the United States to assure our internal security against foreign directed subversion and to put every community in order for maximum productive effort and minimum of waste and unnecessary frictions.

I call upon all loyal citizens to place the nation's first in mind and in action to the end that we may mobilize ready for instant defensive use all of the physical powers, moral strength and all of the material resources of

WITNESS WHEREOF I have hereunto set my hand and caused United States of America to be affixed.

the City of Washington this twenty-seventh day of May, in the year of our Lord nineteen hundred and forty-one, and of the Independence of the United States of America the one hundred and sixty-fifth.

Franklin D Roosevelt

By the President:

Cordell Hull

Secretary of State

Fight For Freedom — World War II

Proclamation of an Unlimited National Emergency (May 27, 1941)
The original official proclamation signed by Franklin D. Roosevelt.

Lent to The Freedom Train by the National Archives

~~SECRET~~

AEL

CSWD
May 6
2:23 AM

URGENT

From: Fort Mills
To: Chief of Staff

No Number May 6, 1942

    For the President of the United States. With broken heart and
head bowed in sadness but not in shame I report to your Excellency
that today I must arrange terms for the surrender of the fortified
islands of Manila Bay (Corregidor) (Fort Hughes) (Fort Drum) and——

NoSig

Note: Remainder of this message being serviced.

Action Copy: SGS

Info. Copies: File

       OPD
       White House
       Comm. Room
       G-2

CM-IN   (5/6/42)   AM 3:00

RECRADED UNCLASSIFIED
ORDER SEC WAR BY TAG/ 7F28

~~SECRET~~

COPY NO.

THE MAKING OF AN EXACT COPY OF THIS MESSAGE IS FORBIDDEN

Last Message from Corregidor (1942)

This is the last radiogram sent from Corregidor by General Jonathan Wainwright to the War Department on
May 6, 1942. The last part of it was garbled and communications were broken before clarification was received.
It remained unsigned.

Lent to The Freedom Train by the War Department

HEADQUARTERS 101ST AIRBORNE DIVISION
Office of the Division Commander

24 December 1944

What's Merry about all this, you ask? We're fighting - it's cold we aren't home. All true but what has the proud Eagle Division accomplished with its worthy comrades of the 10th Armored Division, the 705th Tank Destroyer Battalion and all the rest? Just this: We have stopped cold everything that has been thrown at us from the North, East, South and West. We have identifications from four German Panzer Divisions, two German Infantry Divisions and one German Parachute Division. These units, spearheading the last desperate German lunge, were headed straight west for key points when the Eagle Division was hurriedly ordered to stem the advance. How effectively this was done will be written in history; not alone in our Division's glorious history but in World history. The Germans actually did surround us their radios blared our doom. Their Commander demanded our surrender in the following impudent arrogance.

December 22nd 1944

"To the U. S. A. Commander of the encircled town of Bastogne.

The fortune of war is changing. This time the U. S. A. forces in and near Bastogne have been encircled by strong German armored units. More German armored units have crossed the river Ourthe near Ortheuville, have taken Marche and reached St. Hubert by passing through Hombres-Sibret-Tillet Libramont is in German hands.
There is only one possibility to save the encircled U. S. A. Troops from total annihilation: that is the honorable surrender of the encircled town. In order to think it over a term of two hours will be granted beginning with the presentation of this note.
If this proposal should be rejected one German Artillery Corps and six heavy A. A. Battalions are ready to annihilate the U. S. A. Troops in and near Bastogne. The order for firing will be given immediately after this two hour's term.
All the serious civilian losses caused by this Artillery fire would not correspond with the well known American humanity.

The German Commander

The German Commander received the following reply:

22 December 1944

"To the German Commander:

N U T S !

The American Commander

Allied Troops are counterattacking in force. We continue to hold Bastogne. By holding Bastogne we assure the success of the Allied Armies. We know that our Division Commander, General Taylor, will say: "Well Done!"
We are giving our country and our loved ones at home a worthy Christmas present and being privileged to take part in this gallant feat of arms are truly making for ourselves a Merry Christmas.

McAULIFFE,
Commanding.

"Merry Christmas" from General McAuliffe

On Christmas Eve of 1944, the 101st Airborne Division was completely surrounded by German units.

Just a couple of days before, the Germans realizing that they ostensibly had complete control of the military situation, demanded the surrender of the Division, under the acting command of Brigadier General Anthony C. McAuliffe.

This mimeographed "Greeting Card" was distributed by McAuliffe to his fighting men. We know his famous answer to the German demand for surrender — "NUTS!"

Lent to The Freedom Train by the War Department

ACT OF MILITARY SURRENDER

1. We the undersigned, acting by authority of the German High Command, hereby surrender unconditionally to the Supreme Commander, Allied Expeditionary Force and simultaneously to the Soviet High Command all forces on land, sea, and in the air who are at this date under German control.

2. The German High Command will at once issue orders to all German military, naval and air authorities and to all forces under German control to cease active operations at 2301 hours Central European time on 8 May and to remain in the positions occupied at that time. No ship, vessel, or aircraft is to be scuttled, or any damage done to their hull, machinery or equipment.

3. The German High Command will at once issue to the appropriate commanders, and ensure the carrying out of any further orders issued by the Supreme Commander, Allied Expeditionary Force and by the Soviet High Command.

4. This act of military surrender is without prejudice to, and will be superseded by any general instrument of surrender imposed by, or on behalf of the United Nations and applicable to GERMANY and the German armed forces as a whole.

- 1 -

Germany Surrenders Unconditionally (May 7th, 1945)

The Nazis, who launched the most brutal war the world has ever seen, were brought to their knees in the spring of 1945. It was nearly 3 a.m., 0241 hours, on May 7 at Rheims when the unconditional surrender of "all forces on land, sea, and air" under German control was signed. It provided that military operations were to cease on May 8. This is the original document.

Lent to The Freedom Train by the National Archives

5.   In the event of the German High Command or any of the forces under their control failing to act in accordance with this Act of Surrender, the Supreme Commander, Allied Expeditionary Force and the Soviet High Command will take such punitive or other action as they deem appropriate.

Signed at *Rheims* at *0241* on the *7th* day of May, 1945.
France

On behalf of the German High Command.

Jodl

<u>IN THE PRESENCE OF</u>

On behalf of the Supreme Commander,
Allied Expeditionary Force.

W. B. Smith

On behalf of the Soviet
High Command.

Sousloparov

F. Sevez -2-

Major General, French Army
(Witness)

UNITED STATES SHIP **MISSOURI**

Sunday   2   September , 19 45
(Day)   (Date)   (Month)

00-04

Anchored in berth F 71, Tokyo Bay, in 10 fathoms of water, mud bottom, with 50 fathoms of chain to the starboard anchor on the following anchorage bearings: right tangent Fort #1 168°T, Yokosuka Breakwater Light 325°T, Fort #2 193°T. Boilers #1, #4, #5, and #8 are in use. Condition of readiness III is set. S.O.P.A. is in the U.S.S. SOUTH DAKOTA (BB57). Administrative S.O.P.A. is in the U.S.S. SAN DIEGO (CL53). Various units of the Pacific Fleet and British Fleet are present.

J.H. Hofman
J.H. Hofman, Lt.(jg), U.S.N.

04-08

Anchored as before. 0707, U.S.S. TAYLOR (DD468) came alongside to port with Lt.Col. R. Powell and about 170 press agents to attend surrender ceremonies of the Japanese Imperial Forces. 0733, U.S.S. TAYLOR (DD468) cast off. 0750, exercised crew at quarters for scheduled ceremonies.

M. Olson
M. Olson, Lt.(jg), U.S.N.

08-12

Anchored as before. 0803, U.S.S. BUCHANAN (DD484) came alongside to port with various general officers of the Army and foreign representatives to witness surrender ceremonies. 0805, Fleet Admiral C.W. Nimitz came aboard and his personal flag was broken at the mainmast. 0824, U.S.S. BUCHANAN (DD484) cast off. 0838, U.S.S. NICHOLAS (DD449) came alongside to port with General of the Army Douglas Mac Arthur. 0843, General of the Army Douglas Mac Arthur came aboard and his personal flag was broken at the mainmast alongside the personal flag of Fleet Admiral C.W. Nimitz. 0848, U.S.S. NICHOLAS (DD449) cast off. 0856, Japanese representatives came aboard. At 0902, with the following present, the ceremony commenced and the Instrument of Surrender was presented to all parties:

United States

Colonel Q.S. Lander (SCAP Liaison)

Republic of China

Gen. Hsu Yung-Chang	Vice Adm. Yang Hsuan Chang
Lt. Gen. Chu Shih Ming	Maj. Gen. Wang Chih
Co. Li Sho Chang	Col. Wang Pei Cheng

United Kingdom

Admiral Sir Bruce Fraser	Capt. A.D. Nicholl
Comdr. R.H. Courage	Comdr. (S) A.P. Cartwright
Surgeon Lieut. G.R. Gayman	Lt. V.C. Merry

Representing British Pacific Fleet

Vice Adm. Sir H.B. Rawlings	Commodore J.P.L. Reid
Lt. G.E. Cook	Rear Adm. E.J.P. Brind
Lt. E.B. Ashmore	

United Soviet Socialist Republic

Lt. Gen. Kuzma Nikolaevish Derevyanko	Maj. Gen. Nikolai Vasilevich Voronov
Rear Adm. Andrey Mitrofanovich Stetzenko	Maj. Ivan Joseph Borovsky
Capt. Nikolai Michailovich Karamishev	Lt. Nikolai Nikolaevich Tulinov

Commonwealth of Australia

Gen. Sir Thomas Blamey	Lt. Gen. F.H. Berryman
Rear Adm. George D. Moore	Air Vice Marshall Jones
Air Vice Marshall Bostick	Commodore J.A. Collins
Capt. J. Balfour	

Dominion of Canada

Col. L. Moore Cosgrave

Republic of France

Gen. LeClerc

Commonwealth of New Zealand

Air Vice Marshall Isitt   Lt. J.D. Alfingham

United Kingdom of Netherlands

Adm. Helfrich	Lt. Gen. L.H. Van Oyen
Col. C. Giebel	Comdr. A.A. Fresco

Japanese Empire

Mr. Mamoru Shigemitsu, Foreign Minister	General Yoshijiro Umezo
Katsuo Okazaki	Saburo Ohta
Shunichi Kase	Lt. Gen. Shuichi Miyakazi
Major Gen. Yatsuji Nagai	Col. Kaziyi Sugita
Rear Admiral Tadatoshi Tomioka	Rear Admiral Ichiro Yokoyama
Captain Katsuo Shiba	

APPROVED: EXAMINED:

S.S. Murray   *H.B. Lyon*
S.S. MURRAY, Captain, U.S.N COMMANDING.   H.B. LYON, Commander, U.S.N. NAVIGATOR

TO BE FORWARDED DIRECT TO THE BUREAU OF NAVAL PERSONNEL AT THE END OF EACH MONTH

U. S. GOVERNMENT PRINTING OFFICE: 1944 O - 617906

Log of the "USS Missouri" — Japanese Surrender

The conclusion of the bloodiest war in history was formally marked with the signing of surrender terms by the Japanese in Tokyo Bay, September 2, 1945. The log of the United States battleship "Missouri" for that day is displayed to show the list of Japanese delegates and the representatives of the United Nations including General Douglas MacArthur, Supreme Commander for the Allied Powers, on board to witness the ceremony.

Lent to The Freedom Train by the Navy Department

UNITED STATES SHIP **MISSOURI**

Sunday 2 September , 19 45
(Day) (Date) (Month)

ADDITIONAL REMARKS

08-12 (continued)

U.S. Navy

Fleet Admiral Chester W. Nimitz	Admiral William F. Halsey, jr.
Admiral Richmond K. Turner	Vice Admiral John H. Towers
Vice Admiral John S. Mc Cain	Vice Admiral Charles A. Lockwood, jr.
Vice Admiral Theodore S. Wilkinson	Vice Admiral Frederick C. Sherman
Lt. General Roy S. Geiger, USMC	Rear Admiral John F. Shafroth, jr.
Rear Admiral Donald B. Beary	Rear Admiral Oscar C. Badger
Rear Admiral Howard F. Kingman	Rear Admiral James C. Jones, jr.
Rear Admiral Wilder D. Baker	Rear Admiral Lynde D. Mc Cormick
Rear Admiral Ingram C. Sowell	Rear Admiral Lloyd J. Wiltse
Rear Admiral Gerald F. Bogan	Rear Admiral Robert B. Carney
Rear Admiral Arthur W. Radford	Rear Admiral Donald B. Duncan
Rear Admiral Thomas R. Cooley	Rear Admiral Forrest P. Sherman
Rear Admiral Thomas L. Sprague	Rear Admiral John J. Ballentine
Rear Admiral C.A.F. Sprague	Rear Admiral Carl Holden
Brigadier Gen. Herman C. Feldman, USA	Commodore Oliver O. Kessing
Commodore Joel T. Boone (MC)	Commodore John P. Womble
Brigadier Gen. Wm. T. Clement, USMC	Brigadier Gen. J.H. Fellows, USMC
Commodore Roland N. Smoot	Commodore Roger W. Simpson
Commodore John M. Higgins	Commodore Joseph C. Cronin
Captain Tom B. Hill	Colonel Theodore J. Dayharsh, USA
Captain Harold D. Krick	Captain William D. Anderson
Captain Ralph E. Wilson	Captain Edwin J. Layton
Captain John G. Cross	Captain Fitzhugh Lee
Captain Marion C. Cheek	Captain Herbert L. Hoerner
Captain Arthur H. Taylor	Commander M. Ward
Commander Howell A. Lamar	Major Roy Owsley, USMCR
Lt. Commander Kaufman	Lieutenant Stringer

U.S. Army

General of the Army Mac Arthur	
Maj. Gen. Kean	Maj. Gen. Valdes
Maj. Gen. Ryan	Maj. Gen. Whitlock
Maj. Gen. Sverdrup	Maj. Gen. Bertrandias
Maj. Gen. Willoughby	Maj. Gen. Wurtsmith
Maj. Gen. Byers	Brig. Gen. Chambers
Lt. Gen. Gairdner	Lt. Gen. Whitehead
Maj. Gen. Marshall	Maj. Gen. Swing
Maj. Gen. Frink	Maj. Gen. Chamberlin
Maj. Gen. Stivers	Maj. Gen. Akin
Major Gen. Casey	Maj. Gen. Marquet
General Stilwell	General Krueger
General Hodges	General Spaatz
General Kenney	General Eichelberger
Lt. Gen. Richardson	Lt. Gen. Sutherland
Lt. Gen. Styer	Lt. Gen. Giles
Lt. Gen. Wainwright	Lt. Gen. Percival

and various other general officers. 0904, Mamoru Shigemitsu, Japanese Foreign Minister
signed for Japan. 0906, General Yoshijiro Umezo, Chief of Staff, Japanese Army Headquarters,
signed for Japan. 0908, General of the Army Douglas Mac Arthur, the Supreme Commander for
the Allied Powers, signed for all nations. 0912, Fleet Admiral C.W. Nimitz signed for the
United States. 0913, General Hsu Yung-Chang signed for China. 0914, Admiral Sir Bruce
Fraser signed for the United Kingdom. 0916, Lt.General Kuzma Nikolaevish Derevyanko signed
for the United Soviet Socialist Republic. 0917, General Sir Thomas Blamey signed for
Australia. 0918, Colonel L. Moore Cosgrave signed for Canada. 0920, General LeClerc signed
for France. 0921, Admiral Helfrich signed for the Netherlands. 0922, Air Vice Marshall
Isitt signed for New Zealand. 0925, ceremony completed. 0926, U.S.S. TAYLOR (DD468) came
alongside to port to embark correspondents and photographers. 0929, Japanese representatives
left the ship. 0940, U.S.S. TAYLOR (DD468) cast off. 0945, U.S.S. NICHOLAS (DD449) came
alongside to port to embark General of the Army Douglas Mac Arthur. 0958, General of the
Army Douglas Mac Arthur left the ship and his personal flag was hauled down. 1003, U.S.S.
NICHOLAS (DD449) cast off. 1005, U.S.S. BUCHANAN (DD484) came alongside to port to embark
allied representatives. 1027, U.S.S. BUCHANAN (DD484) cast off. 1044, Fleet Admiral C.W.
Nimitz left the ship. 1052, secured the crew from quarters. 1059, CinCPac's flag was broken
in the U.S.S. SOUTH DAKOTA (BB57). Hauled down CinCPac's flag; broke flag of Commander
Third Fleet.

J. L. Starnes, Jr

J.L. Starnes, Jr., Lt.Comdr., U.S.N.R.

APPROVED:

S.S. MURRAY, Captain, U.S.N. COMMANDING.

EXAMINED:

H.B. LYON, Commander, U.S.N. NAVIGATOR

Headquarters Tenth Army

7 September 1945

Surrender

The undersigned Japanese Commanders, in conformity with the general surrender executed by the Imperial Japanese Government, at Yokohama, on 2 September 1945, hereby formally render unconditional surrender of the islands in the Ryukyus within the following boundaries:

30° North 126° East, thence 24° North 122° East, thence
24° North 133° East, thence 29° North 131° East, thence
30° North 131° 30' East, thence to point of origin.

納見敏郎

Toshiro Nomi
Lieutenant General
Commander Japanese Forces
Sakishima Gunto

高田利貞

Toshisada Takada
Major General
Commander Japanese Army Forces
Amami Gunto

加藤唯雄

Tadao Kato
Rear Admiral
Commander Japanese Navy Forces
Amami Gunto

Accepted: Joseph W. Stilwell,
J. W. Stilwell
General, United States Army
Commanding

Surrender of Japanese Forces in the Ryukyus

General Joseph W. ("Vinegar Joe") Stilwell accepted the surrender of Japanese forces on the Ryukyus Islands on September 7, 1945. This is the original instrument of surrender.

Lent to The Freedom Train by the National Archives

49

For the United Kingdom of Great Britain and Northern Ireland:
Pour le Royaume-Uni de Grande-Bretagne et d'Irlande du Nord:
大不列顛及北愛爾蘭聯合王國:
За Соединенное Королевство Великобритании и Северной Ирландии:
Por el Reino Unido de la Gran Bretaña e Irlanda del Norte:

Halifax.
Cranborne.

For the United States of America:
Pour les Etats-Unis d'Amérique:
美利堅合衆國:
За Соединенные Штаты Америки:
Por los Estados Unidos de América:

E. R. Stettinius Jr.
Cordell Hull
Tom Connally
A. H. Vandenberg.
Sol. Bloom
Charles A. Eaton
Harold E. Stassen
Virginia C. Gildersleeve

The United Nations Charter (1945)

Even before World War II was over, the United Nations met in San Francisco from April 25 to June 26, 1945, to create a new world organization to preserve peace. The Charter that was written and signed in San Francisco was reproduced in exact facsimile by the Department of State and each signatory nation was officially supplied with a copy. This is the United States' official copy. It is bound in gold-embossed blue morocco leather as is the original and bears on the cover the seal of the United Nations. Reproduced here is the signatory page of the United States and Great Britian. Opposite, is the signatory page of the Soviet Union.

Lent to The Freedom Train by the Department of State

FOR THE UNION OF SOVIET SOCIALIST REPUBLICS:
POUR L'UNION DES RÉPUBLIQUES SOVIÉTIQUES SOCIALISTES:
蘇維埃社會主義共和國聯邦:
За Союз Советских Социалистических Республик:
POR LA UNIÓN DE REPÚBLICAS SOCIALISTAS SOVIÉTICAS:

authorized to be made, and, on behalf of the United States of America, should recognize the independence of the Philippines:

NOW, THEREFORE, I, HARRY S. TRUMAN, President of the United States of America, acting under and by virtue of the authority vested in me by the aforesaid act of Congress, do proclaim that, in accord with and subject to the reservations provided for in the applicable statutes of the United States,

The United States of America hereby withdraws and surrenders all rights of possession, supervision, jurisdiction, control, or sovereignty now existing and exercised by the United States of America in and over the territory and people of the Philippines; and,

on behalf of the United States of America, I do hereby recognize the independence of the Philippines as a separate and self-governing nation and acknowledge the authority and control over me of the government instituted by the people thereof under the constitution now in force.

IN WITNESS WHEREOF, I have hereunto set my hand and cause the seal of the United States of America to be affixed.

DONE at the City of Washington this Fourth day of July in the year of our Lord, nineteen hundred and forty-six, and of the Independence of the United States of America the one hundred and seventy first.

By the President:

Dean Acheson

Acting Secretary of State

Harry Truman

JUL 8   11 53 AM '46

Proclamation of the Independence of the Philippines, Signed by President Harry S. Truman (1946)

In granting independence to the Philippine Islands, the United States took a step unparalleled in the history of colonial administration. We remained true to our own history of liberty and self-government and kept our promise to the Filipinos, whose loyal support was so valuable in World War II. For more than 30 years the United States guided the Philippines in the ways of democratic government, and in 1934 the Congress passed the Philippine Independence Act providing for complete freedom 10 years after the inauguration of a new Commonwealth Government. But 10 years later World War II was raging. As soon after the end of that conflict as possible, however, independence was proclaimed. It is fitting that the Proclamation of Independence the original of which, signed by President Truman, is shown was issued on our Independence Day, July 4, 1946.

Lent to The Freedom Train by the National Archives

The American Heritage Foundation
Office of the President

This special volume contains reproductions of the most treasured documents of our American Heritage.

They were assembled into a special collection following World War II and placed aboard the famous Freedom Train. Millions of Americans read their inspiring words as the train traveled throughout the United States. The purpose:

To persuade all Americans that only by active personal participation in the affairs of the nation can we safeguard and preserve our liberties and continue to demonstrate to ourselves and to the world that the way of free men is best.

Now, many years later, the Freedom Train no longer travels throughout our country. But its inspiration and its message are certainly at least as important today as then. Americans cannot take for granted our heritage of freedom. Americans cannot casually accept it as a gift from our forefathers without making every possible personal effort to preserve it.

And we must never forget that today, as always, this vital truth, as expressed in the slogan of the Freedom Train:

FREEDOM IS EVERYBODY'S JOB!

THOMAS D'ARCY BROPHY
President, The American Heritage Foundation